Heart Refined

Heart Refined

My Journey Toward Intimacy With God

Walt Conger

Micah & Jackie,

Thank you so much for all your prayers over the course of the last year.

Walt Conger
Matthew 11: 28-30

CROSSBOOKS
PUBLISHING

CrossBooks™
A Division of LifeWay
1663 Liberty Drive
Bloomington, IN 47403
www.crossbooks.com
Phone: 1-866-879-0502

©2011 Walt Conger. All rights reserved.

No part of this book may be reproduced, stored in a retrieval system, or transmitted by any means without the written permission of the author.

First published by CrossBooks 7/6/2011

ISBN: 978-1-6150-7904-9 (sc)
ISBN: 978-1-6150-7905-6 (hc)

Library of Congress Control Number: 2011930452

Artwork Credit: Craig Pennington
cnpennart@mindspring.com

Scripture taken from the Holy Bible, New International Version®. Copyright © 1973, 1978, 1984 Biblica. Used by permission of Zondervan. All rights reserved.

Printed in the United States of America

This book is printed on acid-free paper.

Any people depicted in stock imagery provided by Thinkstock are models, and such images are being used for illustrative purposes only.

Certain stock imagery © Thinkstock.

Because of the dynamic nature of the Internet, any web addresses or links contained in this book may have changed since publication and may no longer be valid. The views expressed in this work are solely those of the author and do not necessarily reflect the views of the publisher, and the publisher hereby disclaims any responsibility for them.

To Grandma Hill,
The gentlest, kindest and sweetest person I have ever known.
We were sad to see you leave us, but I am looking forward to seeing you again.

Contents

Acknowledgments		ix
Foreword		xi
Chapter 1	Childhood	1
Chapter 2	Marriage	7
Chapter 3	Hearing the Holy Spirit	12
Chapter 4	The Phone Call	17
Chapter 5	Tuesday Night Men's Group	25
Chapter 6	Bikes and Bible	36
Chapter 7	Room of Grace	40
Chapter 8	The Summer of 2010	46
Chapter 9	"Call 911"	50
Chapter 10	The Diagnosis	58
Chapter 11	Surgery	64
Chapter 12	Out of Surgery	69
Chapter 13	Discharged	80
Chapter 14	Recovery	89
Chapter 15	Nine Weeks and Counting	100
Chapter 16	Back to the Hospital	105
Chapter 17	What Now?	116

Acknowledgments

SARAH – THANK YOU FOR ALWAYS being there for me. You have stood by my side through some rough waters, and I thank God daily for bringing you into my life. I love you.

Gabe and Hope – Each one of you is a blessing directly from God. I cannot imagine life without the two of you. I love you both very much.

Mom – You have always shown me unconditional love. Thank you for caring and being there for me. My respect and love for you continues to grow.

Grandpa and Grandma – Who I am today would not have been possible without your consistent love and support. Thank you for being godly grandparents I can look up to. I love you.

Tim – My brother! We have come a long way, haven't we? We both know it is only by the grace of God. Thank you for being there for me.

Foreword

EVER SINCE WALT CAME TO OUR church a few years ago, he impressed us as an active and healthy young husband and father of two. Yet he was just days from a one-hundred-mile bike ride when his whole world turned upside down. After a 911 call and a midnight chopper flight to University Hospitals in Ann Arbor, his life and future was thrust into the hands of a waiting cardiology team. I'll let him tell you about it.

In an age of amazing technological advances, Walt's chance of survival was very slim, yet his recovery has been nothing short of remarkable. But that's not what sets his story apart. What makes his story unique is the procedure the Great Physician has been simultaneously performing in Walt's spiritual heart. Like so many of us in evangelical churches, Walt looked as spiritually fit as he did physically. He dutifully did what good Christians do and abstained from things good Christians abstain from. He faithfully attended services and blended in well with Christian culture. Nothing seemed out of line ... certainly nothing requiring radical measures! But God's spirit had been graciously creating a sense in him that all was not as it could be and should be. The symptoms were internal yet undeniable. James speaks of this God-produced sense of discontentment and longing. "Or do you think Scripture says without reason that the spirit he caused to live in us envies intensely? But He gives us more grace. That is why Scripture says, 'God opposes the proud but gives grace to the humble'" (James 4:5–6). Walt hungered for a relationship with Christ that was deeper, more honest, and more intimate than he had previously known. Through soul discomfort, a valley of physical adversity, and in the fellowship of some honest friends, the Lord is leading him into the intimate relationship He purchased for us.

Like that amazing cardiology team that waited for Walt's arrival, the Lord is waiting. He waits for His children to trade religiosity for an authentic relationship with the Creator-Savior who loves them. He patiently waits for us to sense our need for the relationship we were saved to enjoy. He waits for us to entrust our whole being into His capable hands. And just as Jesus promised, the grace way of relating to God through Jesus isn't burdensome, frustrating, or guilt producing. It's like coming home to rest after a long and hard day at work. *"Come to me, all you who are weary and burdened, and I will give you rest. Take my yoke upon you and learn from me, for I am gentle and humble in heart, and you will find rest for your souls. For my yoke is easy and my burden is light"* (Matt. 11:28–30). Our prayer is that God will use Walt's story to help you discover what it means to let Christ do the heavy lifting as you enjoy what it means to take His yoke upon you.

Dean Stewart, Sr. Pastor
Mayfair Bible Church

Chapter One
Childhood

"The good news is that you are still here with us" is what I heard just before learning that my aorta was dissecting and that I had a slim chance to survive. I was just thirty-eight years old, lying in a hospital bed in Grand Blanc, Michigan. It was 2010, and I had been rushed to the hospital from my home a few miles away, just hours prior to hearing this news. I had this overwhelming sense that I wasn't going to make it, and I prepared myself for the possibility that I might be meeting my Savior. A little over forty-eight hours later, I woke up after surviving an eleven-hour emergency open-heart surgery. Going through a near-death experience such as this made me reflect on my life up to this point, and how I arrived here. I felt led by the Lord to share my journey from childhood up to the present day. I trust that by sharing my journey, you will be able to find some encouragement along the way.

My brother Tim, who is five years younger, and I were raised by our single mom. Our parents divorced when I was six years old and my father moved away when I was eight. My father was a drug and alcohol addict. Because of my father's addictions, I believe the Lord spared me from being in the situation where I had to move between parents. I never gave the situation much thought until much later in life, but, as I get further into my story, it will become clear how vital it was that my father was not in the picture. A verse that I think about many times is Psalm 68:5, which says, "A father to the fatherless, a defender of widows, is God in his holy dwelling."

My grandpa helped fill the void that was left by my father and was instrumental in shaping me into the man I am today. My grandpa served more than just the grandfatherly role. He was also my father, my teacher, and always my hero. He is the one who taught me how to hunt, fish, and play ball, and he installed good godly characters within me. It may have taken a while for those godly characters to come out, but they would play an important role later in life.

My grandma was the perfect image of a godly grandma. She fit the image perfectly of the grandma who would spoil her grandchildren. I remember faking a few illnesses during the school year in order to spend the day at her house, as it would mean a full day of being showered with love and spoiled rotten. I have so many fond memories of my grandma, and she was always concerned about my health. My grandma always tried to get me to drink more water, yet I always resisted. There was one time that I jokingly said that if she paid me, I promised to drink more water. My grandma did not take it as a joke and jumped at the opportunity. She said that I would get paid a nickel for each glass of water that she saw me drink. It did not take very long for the deal to break down, as I quickly cost my grandma several dollars and was prepared to continue drinking as much water as my stomach could handle.

This, however, was not the only time that my grandma listened carefully to what I had to say. One morning, I was being a smart aleck and told my grandma that my favorite dinner was liver and onions. It took a little while, but I succeeded in convincing her that this was indeed the case. My grandma, in her incredible love for me, fixed me liver and onions for dinner that same night. I had to quickly come clean, but it wasn't without having to take several bites of liver and onions. The water and liver and onions incidents showed how much my grandma clearly cared for me. Later on in my story, my grandma will play a vital role in shaping my life and those around me.

I would say that overall I had a quiet, rather non-incidental childhood. However, there is one incident that sticks out. While in the seventh grade, our class won a book-reading contest, which allowed the entire class a day off school. Our house was the last one on the street, and we lived in the country. The house was also up on a steep hill. While alone at home, at around 11:00 a.m., I heard the sound of a car door slamming shut. I peeked out the kitchen window and saw an old beat-up car sitting in the driveway. While looking out the window, I heard a knock at the door. Knowing that I was not allowed to answer the door while at home alone, I kept carefully peeking out the window. After a couple knocks, I saw two scruffy guys walk to the trunk of the car and pull out a crowbar. I quickly ran to a closet and grabbed a shotgun that I used to hunt small game.

The gun was a pump-action twelve gauge. I put a couple shells into the gun and went back into the kitchen. There was a doorway at the far end of the kitchen. Once you opened this door, there was a small entryway and then another door that led to the outside. I was heading to the first door that led to the entryway when I heard a loud crash. I waited for about five seconds and then opened the first door. The door to the outside was opened. There was still a screen door between me and the outdoors. I saw no one there and raised my shotgun. I am not sure why my instinct was to raise the shotgun, but, at nearly the same time that I raised the gun, one of the scruffy guys hopped up on the cement porch that led into the house. To this day, the look on his face is engraved in my brain. It was a look of sheer terror. I am sure that they had spent time scouting the house out and were positive that no one was home. On a normal day, my mom would be working and my brother and I were at school. As soon as I saw him hop up on the porch, I pulled the trigger. There was a click followed by a couple of seconds of what seemed like two minutes, and the guy ran off. They jumped into their car and sped away. I then realized that I had forgotten to rack the shell into the chamber.

I didn't even think to call 911 but rather called my mom at work. I am sure she was terrified and felt helpless. My mom called 911 as well as our church, which was about five miles away. A couple of men from the church arrived quickly, and about a half hour later the police arrived. I remember the police talking individually to the men from the church as well as to my mom, who had now come home from work. A little while later, the policeman spoke to me privately. It was obvious that he thought I was fabricating the story for attention. I clearly remember that the policeman was upset over the part of my story that had me scrambling for the gun so quickly. I am not exactly sure why I did everything in the order that I did other than the Lord was protecting both our house from being broken into, as well as protecting me. We had an old home. The door that was pushed open was old and beat up and the two thieves probably were able to get the door open without using the crowbar. The door did not show any signs of forced entry, probably because it was well banged up to begin with. I know wholeheartedly that God orchestrated the shell not being in the chamber. The muzzle of the shotgun was less than a foot away from the thief's face. If the gun had went off, the results would have been traumatic for me. Even with the gun not going off, it is a story that I remember as if it were yesterday.

My work career began at the ripe age of twelve. There was a horse farm that was run by a Polish doctor within walking distance from my house. During the summer, I would walk down there almost daily and do whatever chores that they needed me to do. The chores mainly consisted of cleaning stalls and exercising horses. From the very beginning, I enjoyed being around horses. Since I started working at the farm at a younger age, I believe this instilled in me a good work ethic.

The school that I attended was part of a church-school combination. I started in the first grade in 1976 and attended this school until the ninth grade. My grandpa, after retiring from General Motors, taught at this same school for a few years. He was well respected as a teacher, and no one was able to get away with much in his classes. The school had a demerit system. If someone was doing something that he or she should not have been doing and was caught, the teacher would give a piece of paper that was called a *demerit*. After so many demerits, disciplinary measures would be taken. My grandpa called these tickets. Instead of wasting his class time going over to his desk, getting a demerit, and handing it to a student, he would quickly stop in the middle of his teaching and simply say to the person that was misbehaving, "Go get a ticket", and would immediately continue teaching. "Go get a ticket" became quite a catchphrase while my grandpa was teaching.

Although I loved having my grandpa as a teacher, I did not receive any special privileges. There was one particular class in which I was sitting in the front row off to the side. I was whispering to the person next to me and carrying on. I assumed that my grandpa could not see me, but was I wrong. All of a sudden, my grandpa stopped abruptly from teaching and called me out. Very sternly he said, "Walt, if you think you are going to get any special privileges while in my classroom, you had better think again. I do not want to hear another word out of you." Let me tell you, I was embarrassed. I wished he had given me a ticket instead. The stern look and the tone of his voice was something I had never heard or seen before. Just writing about this makes my face turn red. Although I was embarrassed and unhappy at the time, I always had the upmost respect for my grandpa.

After the ninth grade, my grandpa made the decision to home-school my brother and me. My grandpa ran a tight ship. We would start on time each morning, and we had to be dressed and ready when he arrived. Although I never had any issues in school that I am aware of, it was helpful to have the one-on-one attention of my grandpa. I always struggled in math, and this was one area that my grandpa excelled in.

My grandpa continued to home-school us for the next three years until I graduated in 1990. I was able to get my diploma from the school that we were working through which was based in Illinois. That was also the year that my mom was remarried to a terrific guy she had been dating for several years.

Chapter Two

✝

Marriage

BETWEEN MY JUNIOR AND SENIOR YEARS in high school I met Sarah, who would eventually become my wife. The way in which we met was unique. We attended rival Christian high schools as well as different churches. Both of our high schools and churches were located near our hometowns in the Flint, Michigan area. While Sarah's parents were away to New York, Sarah was staying with a friend. This friend attended my church, and they both came on a Wednesday night. A few of us went out for a bite to eat after church, and Sarah and I started to date immediately. Sarah's parents were a little shocked when they received a call in New York from the parents of the friend whom Sarah was staying with, seeking permission for Sarah to go out with me. The parents of Sarah's friend vouched for me, and the rest is history.

Shortly after Sarah and I met, and during my senior year of being home-schooled, I contracted mononucleosis. I was very sick for a couple of weeks and remember being happy that Sarah was in my life at the time. She provided much needed comfort during this sickness.

I don't recall thinking too much about college prior to meeting Sarah. The one thing that I was sure of was that I wanted to attend a college close to home and have the ability to work. Meeting Sarah changed those plans.

By the time we graduated, I was definitely in love. Sarah was going away to South Carolina for college, and I was sick about the possibility of being away from her. I decided to attend the same college, and we were off to South Carolina together.

I had absolutely no idea what I wanted to study. Love had a tight grip on me, and I knew that I wanted to be near Sarah as much as possible. Sarah started out by majoring in accounting, so I found a major that had some of the same classes. The major that I picked was operations management. I have to admit that, at the time, I had absolutely no idea what operations management was. All I knew was that I would be in a few classes with Sarah. It did not take long to realize that I was in over my head, and I had to ask Sarah for help way too much, which was not good for our relationship.

In my second year of college, I switched my major to criminal justice and felt that this was something that I would enjoy. My problem was that I did not take college serious enough, and, although I did much better in my new major, I was still struggling academically.

I do have some fond memories of college and met some neat people, but unfortunately the things that stick out the most were a couple of pranks.

Lights were required to be out at 11:00 p.m., and we were supposed to stay in bed. At around 2:30 a.m. one night during my freshman year, my roommate and I decided to get up, sneak to the lobby, and carry all of the furniture into the showers. The idea was not to be destructive but to see the reactions of those that found them sitting in their shower. One of us would serve as the lookout person while the other would grab a piece of furniture and place it in a shower. We took turns doing this. We were almost finished, and up to this point had gotten away with the prank, until my roommate decided to carry a bubble gum machine down the hall. The machine was one with a glass globe. This would have been fine if the bubble gum machine had not been half empty. I can still clearly remember the noise that the machine made as my roommate was running down the hall while the gumballs were banging up and down in the glass globe. Fortunately for me, I was in the room, peaking out the door, and was able to calmly crawl back into bed as my roommate was apprehended by the dorm supervisor.

The other prank that ran rampant in the dorms consisted of a screwdriver and a bottle of shaving cream. During the middle of the night, two people would sneak up to a doorm room. One of the persons would swing the door open while the other would stab the shaving cream can with the screwdriver and quickly throw the can into the room. The result was an area that looked as though a snow blizzard had just attacked.

I did manage to get some studying in, but by the end of my sophomore year my grades were low, and my bill was high.

Between my sophomore and junior years of college, I decided to get a job and not return. It was during this summer that I asked Sarah to be my wife. When the fall of 1992 came, Sarah left for college and I was living at home and working. The first year being away from Sarah was extremely tough, but I made as many trips as I could to see her. It was a thirteen-hour drive, so I didn't get to South Carolina as often as I would have liked.

Over the course of the next two years, I continued working in the private security business, and Sarah finished school. In 1994, within two weeks after graduation, we were married. I mentioned earlier that when I was around the age of eight that my father left the state. I never saw or spoke to my father from that time until several weeks before the wedding. Sometime just prior to the wedding, my brother had managed to track down my father. My brother was just three years old when my father had left, and curiosity had gotten the best of him so he began searching. My brother and father had been able to connect and were able to spend time together. My father was hesitant to contact me for fear of my reaction. However, he wanted to come to the wedding and reached out to me and asked if that would be possible. I obliged, and two weeks prior to the wedding he stayed with me in a little house that I had bought just a few months earlier in the Flint, Michigan area. I can say, without much hesitation, that this was a very awkward couple of weeks. I hadn't seen my father in over fourteen years, and now I was going to be with him, by myself, for the next two weeks. Other than the awkwardness, I don't remember much about the two weeks that my father stayed with me.

My father paid for our honeymoon, which we did not expect and appreciated very much. Once we were back from our honeymoon, and settled in, I had a few conversations with my father. The last conversation that I had was him telling me that he would like to call me once a week and rebuild a relationship. That was the last I heard from him.

At the time that Sarah and I were married, I was attending the church that Sarah had grown up in, and this is where the wedding ceremony was held. On May 21, 1994, Sarah and I were married. We honeymooned in Bar Harbor, Maine, for a week and then came home and started our life together. After we married, we started attending the church where I grew up. My family was currently at this church as well. A few years later, we attended the church where we were married and then ended up back at the church that we attended after getting married.

I was still at the same job in the private security sector that I had been working at since 1992, and, in our fifth year of marriage, Sarah became pregnant with our first child. The pregnancy resulted in a miscarriage as well as other complications. We had to wait a minimum of one year before Sarah could become pregnant again. It was obviously a hard time losing our first child, but I was most concerned with Sarah's health at the time.

In October 1999, we faced the first storm in our marriage. While out of town and riding dirt bikes with my brother Tim, I was involved in a severe accident. Tim and I had just recently purchased new matching Yamaha 225s. We were in the woods during the late morning hour, when the leaves were nice and slick, and were racing. I went around a corner, slipped off the trail, and hit a boulder going about fifty miles per hour. I was behind Tim at the time, so he did not immediately see my accident. A few minutes later, Tim came back and saw that I had been thrown several feet and could not get up to walk. I knew something was horribly wrong. My brother used his cell phone to call 911, and, within a few minutes, the ambulance was back in the woods to load me up. To have an accident such as this, while out of town, and to be sent to a hospital in which you are not familiar, was frightening. I broke my wrist and a couple transverse processes in my back, and had some other injuries.

Once I was home, I had to go visit a hand doctor. It was discovered that I had a very significant break in my wrist and had to undergo wrist surgery in which the surgeon took bone grafts from my right arm and fused them to my right wrist. The surgery was a success, but I will no longer have the ability to fully bend my wrist.

I recuperated well, and in March 2000 I started a new job in the online marketing field. This job allowed me to telecommunicate from home, and I thoroughly enjoyed the new field. In October of the same year, Sarah became pregnant. Our first child, Gabe, was born on June 30, 2001. We were both working full time, and things were going well. A little over two years later, in January 2004, our second child, Hope, was born.

Soon after our daughter was born, the company that I had been working with over the past four years asked Sarah if she would consider working full time with it to help me out with my increased workload. Sarah would be working from home as well. The company had grown significantly, and I had more than I could handle. Sarah had worked in the finance department for seven years for a local public school and enjoyed her job. The decision was difficult, but the company offered to match our current household income and gave some other concessions, which made the decision a little easier. We decided that it was too good of a situation to pass up with having a newer baby at home and the opportunity for us both to be working from home.

I often look back on college, marriage, and having kids and wonder if I knew what I was doing. It makes me realize how God, through His grace, gets us through these times.

Chapter Three

Hearing the Holy Spirit

I was saved at the age of five. I grew up hearing many Bible stories while attending Sunday school classes over the years and assumed that they were simply that: stories. I grew up in a legalistic Christian environment, so I was well aware of all of the rules from a very young age. I knew not to listen to rock music, contemporary Christian music, smoke, drink, say bad words, go to movies, and hang out with those who do.

As I grew into a teen and young adult, I assumed that if I followed the rules as the church and my surroundings had taught me, then I would become a good Christian. The focus was always about what I should *not be doing* and it seemed as if my life was surrounded by that. I don't remember hearing much preaching about listening and following the Holy Spirit and allowing Him to help me do what is right.

As I got older, even into marriage, I continued striving to please God. Although I read very little Scripture at the time, I could never find in the Bible all the rules that I had been brought up to abide by. I had just assumed that if the Christians around me were telling me what I should and should not do, then it had to be correct. I had no idea what it meant to have a relationship with God, how to talk to Him, and how to listen to the Holy Spirit.

Privately, I had no idea why I should not be drinking, going to movies, listening to certain music, wearing jeans to church, etc. I did not feel that all of these things were wrong in and of themselves, and I started to search for answers in the very place that all Christians should be searching. And that is God's Word. As I started looking more into the Scriptures, I began to understand that it is not about trying harder and looking good, but it's about loving God with all your heart and having a relationship with Him. As I grew closer to God, and was sensitive to the leading of the Holy Spirit, I started to shed certain things in my life. In some circumstances, I was hardly noticing that I was losing the desire for them at all. There were priorities in my life that were not biblically wrong, but they had become idols. These idols took my time away from God. As I continued to shed these things, my desire to draw closer to God continued to grow. I started to realize that what I was learning through my relationship with Christ was not lining up with what my church had been teaching me over the years.

I decided to set aside my pride and asked myself this question: Could the beliefs that I have been taught all of these years possibly be wrong?

I began to look around me and realized I was on the cruise ship of Christianity. As long as I did what everyone else expected of me, then things would be calm and cruise along nicely. Instead of seeking my validation from where it should come from—and that is God himself—I was looking to receive my validation from those around me. I was living a poser's life. I was abiding by the rules, but inside I was struggling. I was not reading my Bible or seeking a relationship with Christ and was clearly living what Isaiah 29:13 says: "The Lord says: 'These people come near to me with their mouth and honor me with their lips, but their hearts are far from me. Their worship of me is made up only of rules taught by men.'"

As I look back on these years, I realize that I was right where the enemy wanted me. I was saved and going to heaven, but I was not looking for a relationship with God. It is so hard to explain this life of complacency that I lived. I now know that something much worse was happening to me. I was so consumed with being a good person on the surface that I never realized that I was missing out on an intimate relationship with Christ. Satan does not want Christians to have a relationship with Christ and to be on fire for the Lord, because we then become dangerous.

Early in 2007, the Holy Spirit was speaking to me, and, for the first time in my life, I was listening. Even though we were not happy at the church that we were attending, there was a sense of comfort. It was easy to slip into church and simply blend in. I knew, however, that neither I nor my family could attain any spiritual growth by staying there. After wrestling with the Spirit for a period of time, I spoke to Sarah and we made the decision to start looking for another church. I had attended a very specific type of church throughout my entire life and wanted to use this opportunity to see how other Christians worshipped. We had a few churches on our list. I had grown up in the area, and Sarah had been in the area for a good portion of her life as well, so we both had a really good idea of the types of churches that were around us.

One Sunday morning, Sarah asked if we could go to a church that we had both heard of but was not on our list. The church was a bit of a drive for us, as we were now living in Davison, Michigan, and this particular church was located twenty miles away. That morning, we attended Mayfair Bible Church. I cannot appropriately place into words how incredible that Sunday morning was for us. Everything about the people, the worship, and the message was amazing. We were at a church where the grace of God was abundant, and worshipping God was coming from the hearts. I had an overwhelming feeling that the Holy Spirit had led us to this place, even though I didn't know what all of that meant yet. I did not have much of a prayer life at the time, so I didn't give it the prayer effort that a decision like this deserved, but I did keep myself sensitive to the leading of the Holy Spirit. We attended for about a year, and, in January 2008, we became members of Mayfair Bible Church. To be in an environment where the mission is to learn, love, and live God's Word is where I wanted my family to be. I know that a church cannot in and of itself make you a better person, but God led us to a specific church, and the leading to Mayfair Bible Church was a single step of many yet to come that would have an influence on my life.

At this time, I still did not have a relationship with Christ, but His leading our family to Mayfair Bible Church was the beginning of some powerful changes in my life. Throughout 2008, God really started to get a hold of me, but I was still unsure what to make of it all. What I did know is that I was attending a church that was full of grace, was powerful in worship, and preached the Gospels.

In May 2008, we faced the second storm in our marriage. I had heard rumors that the company that I was working for was receiving offers to be bought. These rumors had been around for awhile, and I was not too concerned. However, late one evening, I got a phone call telling me that the company had been sold, and that Sarah's and my services would no longer be required because for the new owner telecommunicating was not an option. I had indicated over the course of the previous couple of years that we would not be interested in moving, so when the company was sold it did not surprise me that management simply cut ties with us. Just like that, after working with this company for over eight years, both Sarah and I were out of a job. We both had stock options with the company, so that allowed us some time. We were able to pay off bills and put some money away for savings.

Within forty-eight hours, I had another job that also allowed me to telecommunicate from home. We decided that Sarah would be a stay-at-home mom for the time being.

In November 2008, I received an email from a friend of mine from the Lansing, Michigan, area. God was working in his life as well, and he was inviting a few guys to meet weekly in his pole barn. The first meeting was going to be held on Tuesday, January 27, 2009. My friend said that he wanted to provide an atmosphere where guys could get together and share their burdens and struggles. None of us knew what any of this was going to look like or what God was about to do, but God was about to work in each of our lives in some powerful ways.

Chapter Four

✝

The Phone Call

On December 22, 2008, came a phone call from my mom that was the beginning of many life-changing moments. I remember the call as though it was yesterday. I was resting on the couch. It was three days before Christmas, and all the Christmas excitement was in the air. The smells, the decorations, and the anticipation of the children were all evident. As I answered the phone, my mom was on the line and sounded upset, and told me that she had some bad news. My mom proceeded to explain that my grandma, who we all knew was not feeling well lately, had gone to the doctor. My grandma had some tests done, and the results showed that there was a good chance that she had cancer. I remember vividly the sick feeling in my stomach when you know that something bad is happening. All the details were not yet available, and these were preliminary findings. After I hung up the phone, I cried for a few minutes. I got control of myself, and then I called my grandma. My grandma and I spoke for a few minutes about some of the details. There were some more tests scheduled for later in January, and it was a matter of waiting until those tests were conducted. My grandparents lived a couple of miles away, so I had the pleasure of always being near them.

The enemy knew that God was working in my life, because after I received the news about my grandma, the bitterness started to set in. The next thirteen days were some of the darkest days that I have ever experienced in my lifetime. The bitterness that swept in started to create a stronghold on me. I was mad at the world and angry with God for allowing something like this to happen to one of the godliest and most faithful women I knew. I would encounter random bouts of excessive crying. I was caught off guard as to how hard I took the news and what was happening around me. I did a really good job of hiding from everyone what exactly was going on inside me.

Christmas was different that year. My grandparents, parents, brother, and other relatives spent the day at our house. My grandma was tired all the time, but she kept a positive attitude. I wanted to be around her as much as possible.

On Sunday, January 4, 2009, I received a call from my mom that my grandmother was having difficulty breathing. My mom had called 911, and my grandmother was going to be taken to the hospital by ambulance. I received the call at a little after 9:00 a.m. as we were on our way to church. I dropped everyone off at church and quickly drove to the hospital.

By the time that I arrived at the hospital, my grandma was in the emergency room. I remember thinking that she looked good; I guess I had expected worse. We spent most of the day on Sunday, January 4, sitting in the curtain area of the emergency room and waiting for test results. Sarah brought Gabe in to see his great-grandma. I remember spending a few minutes debating whether or not we should allow Gabe in to see Grandma, as he was only seven years old, but at the time she was communicating really well and did not look that bad.

As late afternoon progressed, Grandma started to take a turn for the worse. I think we all had assumed at this point that we were going to receive some more information about the cancer, but we were not thinking that the stay in the hospital would be more than a day.

Around early evening time, my mom and I were outside the area where they were keeping my grandma, and we happened to see one of the doctors working on the case. My mom asked him to be really honest about Grandma's condition. Neither one of us was prepared for what we were about to hear. The doctor explained that along with my grandma's age and the signs that were becoming evident, that this was most likely not going to end very well. The doctors still did not know exactly the nature of the cancer, but the signs were pointing that the cancer was quickly making Grandma's condition a lot worse. The doctor continued to speak with us for a few minutes longer. I remember that the moment he walked away, my mom and I just stood in silence for a moment. We then shared our mutual feelings of surprise regarding what he had just said.

As we got into the evening time on Sunday, Grandma continued to get worse, and she was now having a hard time communicating. We were told that she would be admitted and we continued to wait for a room. By late Sunday night, Grandma was in a room and was not doing well at all. Everyone was exhausted. Considering the emotional wear and tear of the day, my grandpa, at eighty-five years of age, was doing well. We all went home for the night to get some rest, except for my mom, who stayed at the hospital so that she could stay close to my grandma.

I did not sleep well on Sunday night and was really struggling with all that was going on. I got up early on Monday morning and by 8:30 a.m. was on the road back to the hospital. When I was about five miles into my drive, I received a call from my mom. I could tell that my mom was very upset. She asked if I was on my way to the hospital and I told her that I would be there shortly. As my mom started to cry, she told me how we almost lost Grandma twice the previous night. At approximately 2:00 a.m., my mom was called into my grandma's room. She was slipping away and the nurses were trying to settle her down. My grandpa and grandma had made it clear that there were to be no methods of resuscitation if it ever came down to that. The nurses were asking my mom if she was sure that this was still the case, and my mom reassured them that it was my grandpa's and grandma's wish. My grandma was able to settle down and lived. At 5:00 a.m., my mom again was called into my grandma's room. She was having difficulties yet again and was close to passing away. For a second time, she made it through and was able to settle down. At this point, my mom was asked to stay in my grandma's room.

This is the moment when reality hit that my grandma might not make it out of the hospital. Prior to that particular phone call, I don't remember thinking that my grandma might not live. I was still under the assumption that the cancer was starting to act up, and some difficult times may be ahead of us, but that she was still going to come home. All that we knew up to this point was a little bit of information from the December 22 results. The additional tests were schedule for later in the month.

Monday was a long day. Grandma was not doing well at all; she was not able to communicate and was unresponsive. We contacted my uncle in Florida and told him that he should make arrangements to come to Michigan. He was able to schedule a flight for the following afternoon. During the day, a good family friend of my grandparents visited. He read one of my grandma's favorite Bible passages: Psalm 23.

> The Lord is my shepherd; I shall not be in want. He makes me lie down in green pastures, he leads me besides quiet waters, he restores my soul. He guides me in paths of righteousness for his name's sake. Even though I walk through the valley of the shadow of death, I will fear no evil, for you are with me; your rod and your staff, they comfort me. You prepare a table before me in the presence of my enemies. You anoint my head with oil; my cup overflows. Surely goodness and love will follow me all the days of my life, and I will dwell in the house of the Lord forever.

My grandma's family doctor visited and told us that Grandma was going to be moved to another room in a section of the hospital where patients go toward the end of their lives to be kept comfortable. Late in the day on Monday, January 5, 2009, Grandma was moved.

During our time in the hospital, my brother Tim and I had a lot of time to talk. We had not been very close over the last several years. Tim had dealt with a lot with drug and alcohol addictions, and we did not have a lot in common. We would get together during family functions and occasionally would be together at times during the hunting season, but we were not very close. It was nice to get the opportunity to have Tim, Grandpa, our mom, and me all together for an extended period of time, even under the circumstances.

As Monday progressed, it was becoming obvious that God was using this time to start working in our lives. The Holy Spirit was working in both my life as well as Tim's life. It is so difficult to appropriately explain what was taking place within me, but God does work in mysteries ways. John 13:7 says, "You do not realize now what I am doing, but later you will understand." That is what I believe was happening here. God was moving in a powerful way, but He was not allowing me to understand it completely.

One of the first areas that God was dealing with in me was my bitterness. I had come into the hospital a bitter person. I was mad at God for what was happening to my grandma, and I assumed that whatever was going to take place while at the hospital was going to make me that much more angry. The result, however, was that the Holy Spirit was working in me and removing the bitterness. I had that sense that God was telling me, "Walt, I got this. This is not taking me by surprise. Allow me to work. Listen to me."

Monday, January 5, 2009, was the day that I can point to when I first got real with God and started listening and talking to Him. The relationship that I longed for with my God started on this day.

My mom and I spent the night in Grandma's room. Tim took my grandpa home and stayed with him that night. There were some precious conversations that took place that evening between my mom and me and between Tim and our grandfather. Obviously none of us slept well. Tim and Grandpa arrived at the hospital early Tuesday morning.

There was a steady stream of visitors on Tuesday morning. My grandma was getting closer to death, and we were told that it would only be a matter of time. We decided to put a sign on the door that indicated that only immediate family members were welcome at this time. As I look back at these last hours, as difficult as they were, I could sense the Holy Spirit working in my life. I felt that God was there, and He was pulling me close to Him and providing me with much needed comfort. Isaiah 41:13 says, "For I am the Lord your God, who takes your right hand and says to you, Do not fear." I felt as though God had my right hand.

Toward the last hours of my grandma's life, my grandpa, mom, stepfather, brother, grandma's sister, Sarah, and I had all taken vigil next to my grandma's bedside. Over the course of the last several hours, there had been a steady stream of visitors. However, our last moments with her were uninterrupted. Psalm 29:11 proclaims, "The Lord gives strength to His people; the Lord blesses his people with peace."

As my grandma was getting much closer to slipping into eternity, my grandpa asked if we could all hold hands so that he could pray. I was in disbelief that while his wife of sixty-four years was lying there ready to slip away, he had the strength to pray. With what could only be by God's power, my grandpa prayed and asked for release of my grandma. My grandpa continued the prayer by telling God that he was ready to let go of my grandma and see her go into heaven. I was overwhelmed with the strength that my grandpa was displaying and knew that God was in the room with us, providing much needed comfort.

At 12:04 p.m., on January 6, 2009, within minutes of my grandpa's prayer, Grandma went peacefully into the presence of the Lord. After a couple minutes of Grandma's passing, my grandpa again prayed and thanked the Lord for His answer to prayer.

Being at a relative's bedside at their passing is a life-changing experience, and this made a very large impact on my life. My grandma was a faithful servant to the Lord, and a wonderful mom, grandma, sister, and wife. I believe that the Lord spared her from all the tests and procedures normally given to cancer patients and ushered her quietly into heaven as a reward for her many years of faithfulness to Him. There is a passage in Isaiah 57:2 that reminds me of the peaceful death of my grandma. The verse says, "Those who walk uprightly enter into peace; they find rest as they lie in death."

As we all sat there for several minutes, crying and hugging, I went out to get a nurse. I called the funeral home to come and take my grandma, as well as to set up a time to meet and go over all the arrangements. My aunt and uncle were in flight at the time that Grandma passed, and we did not look forward to telling them that they were not able to make it on time.

After the funeral home's ambulance had come and left, Sarah and I went home. I left the hospital that day a different person. I walked in on Sunday without a relationship with Christ, and left less than seventy-two hours later a man who had become sensitive to God and had a changed heart. I did not realize it at the time, but God was going to use these seventy-two hours to radically change both my and Tim's lives.

A little later, Tim and my grandpa went to the airport to pick up my aunt and uncle and had to break the news to them. They all went to my grandpa's house and soon I joined them there. I broke down when I saw my uncle. We spent some time talking and sharing stories.

We had very little time until we had to leave for the funeral home to make all the arrangements. The entire ordeal seemed like it was in slow motion. Just a few hours earlier we were sitting at my grandma's bedside, and already we were at the funeral home. I had never had to deal with this situation before, and it was very difficult. We made all the necessary arrangements and went out for dinner afterward.

I had a friend that attended my grandpa's and Grandma's church and he had a good voice. My grandma loved every time he sang in church, so I contacted him and he agreed to sing at the funeral. One of my grandma's favorite songs was "It Is Well with My Soul" and we decided that this would be sung at the funeral. The next several days were spent at the funeral home and at the church for the service. Everything had happened so quickly, and I had a difficult time soaking in the last several days.

At the same time that I was gripped with the emotions over everything that was happening, I could continue to feel God bringing me closer to Him. Leading up to the hospital stay, I was still that stale, complacent, bitter Christian. The enemy could have used my grandma's death to get a further hold on me, but God is much more powerful than that. Instead, the Lord was using my grandma's death for His glory.

The day of my grandma's funeral, a good friend of mine, Tim from Lansing, Michigan, had been rushed to the hospital with meningitis and was gravely ill. As soon as my grandma's funeral was over, Sarah and I left and made the one-hour trip to visit Tim in the hospital. His story in and of itself is amazing. God saved his life, and I am glad to say that he made a full recovery.

Tim's illness was another piece of the puzzle that was used to bring me into a closer relationship to Christ. Being in the ICU and seeing Tim lying there clinging to life so soon after seeing my grandma pass away was very difficult, but I could sense that God was up to something special.

I cannot fully explain why God used my grandma's death and the circumstances surrounding it to begin pulling me closer to Him, but God works in amazing ways, and He used those seventy-two hours to place me on a path to begin a relationship with Him.

Chapter Five

Tuesday Night Men's Group

AFTER THE FUNERAL, MY BROTHER AND I started to communicate a lot more. God was working in my heart. The Holy Spirit was stirring me from within, and I was ready to start reaching out to God, and I yearned for a relationship with Him. I could see that Tim was wrestling with the Lord as well. I invited Tim to the men's group that was starting on January 27. I had never participated in any men's groups, Bible study groups, or other similar groups prior to this, so I had no idea what to expect.

On January 27, Tim and I hopped in the car and began our one-hour trip to the men's group in Lansing. I was sensitive to the Holy Spirit and was excited about this meeting. Tim and I had a good time talking on the way to the group. We were starting to grow closer to one another as we now had something in common, which was the Spirit working in both of our lives.

Just before 7:30 p.m., we arrived. We met in my friend's pole barn. As we walked into the room, I remember thinking how much this looked like *the ultimate man room*. It had a pull-down projector screen, several chairs, and a couch. I felt comfortable being there from the beginning. There were nine of us that first night. The room was not very big, and we were shoulder to shoulder.

My friend started the night by explaining that we were not going to have an agenda. We were going to let the Holy Spirit lead and allow us to share whatever was in our hearts.

A guy by the name of Jon was asked to share his "story." Jon happened to be sitting next to me and what took place over the next several minutes impacted me greatly. To this day, I can still recall Jon's story and the passion with which he told it. I had never heard anything so real and raw in my life.

Jon's story consisted of growing up as a missionary kid and how he had gotten away from the Lord. He had recently come back to Christ and was so passionate about serving Him that it had a tremendous impact on each of us listening to his story.

Over the next several weeks, it became obvious that Jon was our warrior in the group. Jon is the guy that I would want praying for me. If any of us were ever being attacked by the enemy, Jon was the guy to call. Jon was so bold and powerful while praying, and I would always look forward to hearing him pray. As the weeks went by, I grew closer to Jon, and he would reach out to me many times; he had a large impact toward my passion for Christ. To this day, I have saved several emails from Jon. He loved the Psalms, and many of these emails have Psalms quoted in them.

For the first time in my life, I felt like I was in an environment where I could open up about what was going on in my life. Prior to my grandma being sick, I had no relationship with the Lord, and the enemy used that situation to drive me to bitterness. The enemy could have gained a bigger stronghold on me with the death of my grandma, but the Holy Spirit used that trial to start a work in my life. I was in the process of trying to straighten this out, and was anxious to speak to someone about it, but, until I came into contact with this real and raw group of guys, I had no idea where to go.

As I mentioned earlier, my brother Tim had been dealing with some addictions himself. His story of surrender and how he has given his life to

Christ has made a large impact on me, and therefore is a big piece to the puzzle of my life's journey. Tim's story is best told by him, and I asked him if he would write his story down. Allow me to share it with you.

Surrender:
1. To relinquish possession or control to another because of demand or compulsion.
2. To give up in favor of another.
3. To give up or abandon.

    That is ultimately what my story is about: Surrender. How I came to surrender is my story.

    During the first week of January 2009, my grandmother was hospitalized for cancer. I stayed with my grandpa for a couple of days while taking him to and from the hospital. It was during those two days that God began to soften my heart.

    I had struggled with drugs and alcohol since the age of fifteen. When my grandma was hospitalized for cancer, I had been free from drugs for three years. Once I had stopped taking drugs, I quickly replaced the drugs with alcohol.

    So here I was, on my grandpa's couch, waiting for morning so that I could take him to the hospital to see my grandma. I had not had a drink for a couple of days, and because of this I was not sleeping or feeling well.

    When morning finally arrived, I asked my grandpa how he had slept. His answer to that question is one that I will never forget. My grandpa replied, "I couldn't sleep right away, so I lay in bed and talked to God for a couple hours."

I wasn't sure how to respond to that. I was, admittedly, a little angry for how simple he made talking to God sound, so I asked him want he meant by "talked to God." My grandpa explained to me that it was not about religion, or even about church, but more about having an intimate relationship with God. I saw this intimate relationship with God firsthand over the course of the next several days.

My grandma would pass away a couple of days later. Watching my grandpa through the process of losing his partner of sixty-four years, and the peace he had through it all, was nothing short of amazing. God used this whole situation to speak to me about what it looks like to walk with Christ.

Later that same month, my brother Walt invited me to go to a men's meeting that a friend of his was having. Apparently this meeting was going to be in this person's pole barn. Walt explained to me that a few guys were going to get together and talk about things that were going on in their lives, and be supportive of one another. I agreed to check it out but was both intimidated as well as skeptical. In my mind, I pictured a bunch of theological fatheads spewing Scripture, mostly out of context, and trying to fix one another. It didn't take me very long to realize how wrong I was.

What I found was a bunch of guys that loved the Lord and had a desire to get real and honest with each other, and they wanted to put Christ in the center of it all.

I continued to attend for the next several weeks without saying much. I was simply trying to wrap my head around everything that I was witnessing. I convinced myself that if I let these guys get to know the real person that I was—the raging alcoholic—they probably would not want me in their group. I was hearing a lot of amazing stories about some things that the guys were struggling with, but I was still convinced that no one in that room could ever relate to me.

One night changed all of that. A guy in the group, who had been relatively silent up to this point, spoke up and shared his story. For the first time I realized that there was someone in here that could relate to me. I felt as though this guy would understand my struggles, and I was able to understand his struggles. As the evening was coming to a close, I scooted to the edge of the seat and proceeded to tell the guys what I was struggling with. I even told them that I had a drunken binge just two days ago. After a minute of frightening silence, the men stood up, circled around me, and began to pray. I felt emotion like I had never felt before. I could never see me in a room with a bunch of men weeping, but here I was.

I attended the meetings regularly for the next several months. I began to open up and learned what it meant to have a relationship with other believers and, more importantly, with God. The guys help me realize that I could change and repair the relationship with my wife and daughters that had been tarnished by my selfishness. I still wanted to be that guy who could have a cocktail or two and be all right, and the group helped me realize that I just wasn't *that* guy. The guys prayed and emailed me regularly when I needed it the most.

Things finally came to a head on Labor Day weekend, 2009. I was drunk and being unruly toward my family again. When I woke up the following morning, and found out what I had done, I got very angry with myself. I shared what I had done with the guys at the next meeting. They prayed for me and encouraged me to tell God exactly how I was feeling.

On September 9, 2009, I cried out to God. I asked God why I continued to hurt the ones I love, and told God that I would rather hurt myself. I asked, "Why can't I get into a drunk-driving accident or something?" I cried out to God and asked him why I couldn't stop.

After I cried out to God, I heard the word *surrender*. I wasn't sure why the word *surrender* popped into my head, but there it was. I remember asking God if that is all that He wanted.

Right then and there, I told God, "I surrender my addiction to you, I surrender myself to you, and it is yours, God."

After I finished surrendering and talking to God, I realized that I had been talking with God for two hours. For the first time in my life, I felt peace.

I have been clean and sober ever since that day. I am on a journey, a journey of growing in my relationship with Christ and repairing my relationship with my family. It is a journey that I enjoy.

I realize that there will be people out there that will be skeptical of my seemingly overnight conversion, but I attribute my conversion to the power of the Almighty God. I know that God has the power to take my surrender and give me power to rid myself of my addictions.

God used the death of my grandma, along with a group of ragamuffin men, to bring me to a relationship with Him. I look forward to the journey ahead and for the opportunity for God to use me however he sees fit.

- Tim Conger

The men met every Tuesday night. We started to form bonds with one another, and each of us could sense the Holy Spirit at work as we shared the junk in our lives with one another. We prayed for one another, and kept in constant contact with each other. There were so many issues that we were dealing with, and it was refreshing to share those struggles, shine a bright light on the circumstances, bring them forward, and allow God to use each of us to tackle head on what we were going through. It was refreshing to be in a group that did not have a weekly agenda. Many of us had been in groups and studies through the years that stuffed God in a box. One of the purposes of this group was to let God out of that box and allow Him to work through each of us in powerful ways.

I was asked to share my story during week two. When my night came, I shared how bitter I was upon learning of my grandma's illness and explained the best I could what God was doing in my life. I was relieved to be able to share my story and to get out in the open some of the things that I had been struggling with. The guys were extremely supportive and were a great encouragement to me.

In March 2009, we held a surprise "Man" party for Jon. This particular Tuesday marked the one-year anniversary in which Jon had turned his life around for Christ. Some gifts were given, along with dog tags and a sword from the group. Many of us shared how Jon had impacted our lives and the encouragement that he had been to us. It was obvious that Jon was surprised and humbled by the attention. We took a group picture with Jon holding the sword. I love this picture and cherish it greatly.

As the weeks went on, our group grew closer together and became stronger as a unit. Week after week, we would share with each other what we were struggling with at that particular time, and each of us was there for one another. Proverbs 28:13 says, "Whoever conceals their sins does not prosper, but the one who confesses and renounces them finds mercy."

In February 2009, Jon emailed us regarding a homeless person that he had come in contact with while walking during his lunch break. Jon, being someone who loves to share the Gospels, asked the homeless guy if he would like to go and get something to eat. As they were eating, Jon asked him to share *his* story. Jon believes that homeless person accepted Christ that day.

Several weeks later, there was an article in the paper about a homeless guy that had died in an abandoned van that had caught on fire. Sure enough, it was the same person that Jon had spoken to. Jon made some phone calls and spoke to an official with Veterans of America where this homeless person had stayed. At the end of March, they were having a small ceremony for the homeless person, and Jon was asked to say a few words. Our group got together and attended the small service at the Veterans of America facility. A preacher said that if anyone would like to come forward and talk to him, that he would be available. Two homeless people who were there came forward to dedicate their lives to Christ. After the service, we hung around for a little while and talked to some of the homeless people staying at the shelter. Jon, as always, was seeking out people to share what God had done in his life. My brother was there as well and made a connection with a homeless person. The homeless person had shared a little bit of his story with my brother, and it impacted my brother greatly. Not only were we able to see the impact of being open and sharing our stories with each other, but it was beginning to make us sensitive to the stories of others as well. The evening at the shelter had a large impact on all of us.

During the first couple of months of being in the group, I started having the desire to jump off the cruise ship of Christianity that I had been on for so long. I had the desire to hop over to the battleship, sword in hand, and join others on the front lines for Christ. I was coming alive along with those around me and was asking God to continue to use me in any way that He desired. I was ready to start trusting God.

We continued meeting weekly throughout the winter and tackled the many issues that we all were facing head on. We were rallying around one another, praying over each other, and coming alive as a group. Ecclesiastes 4:12 says, "Though one may be overpowered, two can defend themselves. A cord of three strands is not quickly broken."

I started to realize the importance of listening and being sensitive to the Holy Spirit and surrounding myself with men who had the same desires.

By this time, we had a nickname for our group: the Bulls. Someone in the group located a clip on the Internet that depicts a herd of bulls that had separated from a smaller bull. A pack of lions took advantage of the situation and attacked the lonely bull. It appeared that they had the bull smothered, when all of a sudden the rest of the bull herd came to the rescue of the lonely bull. The moral of the video clip was that if we as men are left alone in isolation, it is much easier for the enemy to take us out. When we see one of our own being attacked, we rally together and pray and support that person. Ever since we watched the video tape, the nickname Bulls has stuck.

One weekend in June 2009, the Bulls retreated up north to relax and spend some good quality time together. My brother and I arrived on a Friday afternoon. All together, eighteen of us were present at the first official Bulls retreat. On Friday night, we honored my friend who had started the group. He is a Vietnam War veteran. During the war, he was a radioman, so we all pitched in and bought him an authentic Vietnam backpack radio. We presented him with the radio and spoke about how he was now a radioman in the Lord's army. He is battling on the front lines for Christ and radios in for help when someone needs air support. It was a great time honoring a great man.

We enjoyed a huge supper followed by a time of relaxation around a bonfire. Friday evening was a great time of fellowship, and many great stories were told. There was a lot of reflection on what God was doing in each and every one of our lives.

On Saturday morning, we woke to a fantastic breakfast that consisted of blueberry waffles, bacon, and toast. After stuffing ourselves, we had a great time of prayer, worship, and communion. Later on that day, a few of us decided to get baptized in the lake. I was baptized as a young child but later in college rededicated my life to the Lord. I wanted baptism to be a time that I can remember and wanted to be able to reflect on my obedience to Christ. I was honored to be baptized by two great friends, and then one of the same friends asked if I would baptize him as well. The whole experience was incredible, and the many pictures that we took reflect the joy that we all had that day. The rest of the day on Saturday consisted of swimming, more relaxing, another large supper, and more fellowship around the campfire. I went to bed on Saturday night excited about what God was doing in my life, and appreciative of the fellow warriors that He had led me to. I cannot help but think of Philippians 4:6, which says, "Do not be anxious about anything, but in everything, by prayer and petition, with thanksgiving, present your request to God."

On Sunday morning, we woke up, had some breakfast, did a little canoeing and skeet shooting, and then headed home. It was important for me to be able to see all of us on fire for Christ while having fun at the same time. This first retreat is something that I will never forget.

As the rest of the summer and spring continued on, God kept doing amazing things in our group, and our numbers started to grow.

Our group faced a trial in November 2009. One of the guys, who had been with the group from the beginning, had a stroke. He was rushed to the hospital on a Tuesday night and lay unconscious in intensive care while hooked up to a ventilator. I had the opportunity to visit and pray with him. On Wednesday, he had emergency brain surgery to remove a clot in his brain stem. By Thursday, he was eating and in good spirits. As we all continued to pray for his recovery, he was out of the hospital on Friday. Three days after a stroke, and two days removed from brain surgery, he was able to go home. When he finally made it back to the group, it was exciting to hear his story and testimony and how God was using his trial to do amazing things in his life as well as in the lives of those around him.

As 2009 closed, the group continued to grow, and God continued to do amazing things.

Chapter Six

Bikes and Bible

From June 2009 until the end of the year turned out to be a whirlwind. Sarah and I were invited to a friend's wedding in Las Vegas. Sarah had never been to Vegas before, and we were looking forward to spending a few days of alone time together. The wedding was on June 22, 2009. We flew into Vegas late on Friday evening. I surprised Sarah by having a Town Car waiting to take us to our hotel. By the time we arrived at the hotel, it was extremely late and we were very tired. I opened up my suitcase to unpack it and did not see the new suit coat that I had recently purchased for the wedding. As Sarah was getting ready for bed, I asked her if she had my jacket. She gave me this terrifying *Are you kidding me?* look. We had forgotten to pack it. First thing on Saturday morning, I called my mom and had her ship me the jacket overnight. Of course, it was very costly, and the front desk person expected a hefty tip just to walk into the back room and get my package that I had already paid a large amount for.

We were certainly relieved to have the jacket and spent the day sightseeing. On Saturday afternoon, we went and saw the comedic ventriloquist Terry Fator in concert. Later, we had dinner with our friends who were getting married plus their family and other friends. We spent Sunday sightseeing and took in a Cirque du Soleil show. By Sunday evening, we were worn out from all the walking that we had done in the past couple of days.

Monday was the day of the wedding. It was a beautiful ceremony held in the garden at Caesars Palace. It was a cooler than normal evening for Vegas, so even though it was the end of June the heat was bearable. The ceremony was quick, and we were off to the reception. We had a great dinner and really had a good time. We met new people and Sarah and I enjoyed our time together. We were up bright and early on Tuesday to catch a late-morning flight. We had a relaxing time together, experiencing something new.

In August 2009, I made a commitment to read the complete Bible and to read it daily, as well as commit myself to consistently reading good books. More importantly, my commitment to reading the Bible was not just to be able to say that I completed the entire Bible, but rather to experience a closeness to God that can come while being in the Word every day. I was not prepared for the positive effect that this would have on my life. As I mentioned early in my story, I had hardly ever opened my Bible outside of church. As I read through the Scripture, I kept a daily log of how God would be speaking to me on that particular day. It has been a blessing to look back at the beginning and see how God was working in my life.

As I was committing myself to prayer and daily Scripture reading, I was also telling God that I was ready to serve Him in whatever capacity that might be. I specifically told Him that I was willing to serve my church. Whether that would be by working in the kitchen or cleaning toilets, I didn't care. I just wanted to be a part of God's work. I had never had a willingness to serve in the past, but my desire to serve God was growing.

The very next day, after a very specific prayer about serving, I received a letter in the mail from my church. The letter was from the nominating committee, asking if I would be willing to be on the ballot to serve as a deacon. I specifically remember staring at the letter for several minutes before asking God if He was joking. Less than twenty-four hours after telling God that I was willing and wanting to serve, He was opening doors in ways that I had not thought of. I talked to God about this and was as honest as I could have been. I told Him that I did not feel worthy enough to serve in certain capacities. Less than a year earlier, I was a complacent, inactive Christian. I struggled mightily with this decision, as I took it very seriously. My relationship with Christ was growing, and He reminded me that He could use me in any way that He saw fit. I accepted the nomination but was not elected. God taught me some valuable lessons through this process and showed me how to come to Him for decisions and to accept the outcome, whatever it might be.

In September, an eighty-mile bike trip with my three brothers-in-law was planned. I had been training long and hard for this and was looking forward to the challenge. The four of us met at the house of my brother-in-law, Jon, on a Saturday morning in Grand Rapids, and we were full of anticipation for the trek that was ahead of us. We had a long haul through the city before we arrived at the beginning of the bike path that would take us most of the way into Muskegon. Once we hit the beginning of the trail, we had some lunch and talked about the trip we were about to embark on.

Soon enough, we were on our way. It was a beautiful sunny day. It was very hot, and there were several parts of the trail that were wide open, which allowed the sun to beat down on us. I didn't seem to mind too much in the beginning, but, once we got about twenty-five miles into the trip, it was getting difficult. We kept ourselves hydrated well. The eighty-mile round trip turned into more than fifty miles one way before we arrived at our hotel in Muskegon. Near the end of day one of our trip, we nearly perfected the art of drafting. We were exhausted, but the feeling of accomplishment took the sting off a bit.

The plans were to check into our hotel, shower, and ride to a nearby restaurant for dinner. After speaking to the front desk clerk, we realized that there was not a restaurant nearby. After being on our bikes for several hours, none of us felt like getting back on the bike for a long ride to dinner. We settled into our rooms and mutually decided to take a cab out to dinner. This turned out to be a wise decision, because by the time we arrived at the restaurant and started relaxing, the pain and agony were slowly sinking in. I will have to say that my bottom was as sore as I can ever remember it being.

We enjoyed a nice dinner and good fellowship and took the cab back to our hotel. We watched a little television and were soon ready for a good night's sleep. On Sunday morning, after we had gotten up and around, we had a time of devotions together. I do not take it for granted that all three of my brothers-in-law are godly men, and I was honored to be able to have a good time worshipping the Lord together.

My bottom was so sore on Sunday morning that I was dreading having to get back on the bike for another fifty-mile ride. Sunday was another beautiful day. We did not push too hard on our trip back to Grand Rapids, and leg two of the bike trip went along without incident. We were all thankful that there were no mechanical issues as well as no injuries. Once we got back to the starting point, I was feeling good and had a huge sense of accomplishment. We enjoyed our time together, and I do appreciate my brothers-in-law.

In the previous ten months, I had dealt with some strong bitterness in learning of my grandma's illness, the death of my grandma, a radical change in my life, getting involved with the men's group, seeing a good friend in the group nearly die of a stroke, cycling one hundred miles with my brothers-in-law, and being nominated for deacon. I was overwhelmed with all that was happening but was excited at seeing how God was going to continue to work in my life.

Chapter Seven
✝
Room of Grace

DURING THE MONTHS OF SEPTEMBER AND October 2009, God was really moving in me and giving me a strong burden for men. I saw what the Holy Spirit was doing in our Tuesday night men's group and knew that men were hurting and desired to have a place to share their struggles. In October, through the leading of the Spirit, I set up a meeting with my pastor. One of the first books that I read, after making my book-reading commitment, was a book on grace. I met with my pastor and shared my passion for men.

The passion continued to grow, and, as I felt led, I spoke to more people about it. Shortly after sharing what God was laying on my heart with my pastor, I found myself sharing with another man from the church. One Wednesday evening that month I let it all out regarding my burden for men and providing an atmosphere of grace. Evidently, I made an impact on this man, and I was unaware that he was a part of the church's men's ministry committee. We had a few more conversations about possibly having a ministry called the Room of Grace at Mayfair Bible Church. Since then, he has become a dear friend of mine and has been there for me through many struggles.

My brother knew about this passion that I had for men and had been sharing my passion with his pastor. In December 2009, my brother's pastor asked if I would like to meet with him and simply share the passion that I was feeling. On Christmas Eve, 2009, we met.

I shared in the most honest way that I knew how. I told him about the freedom that men were gaining in our Tuesday night group and how there were men struggling everywhere. I was feeling led by the Holy Spirit to start a group in our area and to try to open up more doors to allow men to share and love and pray with each other.

Once I was finished sharing my passion as strongly as I could, I was asked if there was anything that he could do for me. I told him that if I had a place to meet, then I would work on getting a group started. The church was offered to me as a place to meet. I was so grateful and saw it as the Lord opening a big door.

Later, a beginning date was decided. Below is the letter that I wrote and sent out on January 26, 2010, to several men.

Men,

Many of you know the impact that my Tuesday night men's group in Bath, MI has had on my life. We started just over a year ago, and I am very thankful to the Lord for leading me to this group. It has been amazing to see the surrender and freedom that God has given men by having a group of guys to get together with on a weekly basis and share our burdens, struggles, pray for one another, and to hold each other accountable. Through the year, the Lord gave me a strong passion for men as I continued to see the freedom that came to men's hearts by being together, being real, raw and transparent with one another.

Beginning on Thursday, February 11 at 7:30 p.m., the "Room of Grace" men's group will begin. For those of you who have been involved in men's groups in the past, this will be different than what you may be use to. I am looking for guys that have a heart to be real, raw, and honest, with no posing. The "Room of Grace" is a safe place. Here, you will be respected, not rejected, for sharing whatever "Stuff" you may be dealing with.

I would love to see you come out, as I believe it will be an encouraging time for all of us, and I am looking forward to being encouraged from each and everyone one of you. If you can make it out, great, if not, that is fine. The "Room of Grace" will be available each and every Thursday. Come as you can.

I prayed a lot for the Room of Grace over the next couple of weeks. I felt that the Lord was leading me to do this, and I expected the enemy to attack. I was not prepared for the attacks that came. A couple of weeks before the Room of Grace was to begin, the attacks intensified, and I was being fed lies from the enemy. Some of the lies I was hearing from the enemy were:

1. You're not good enough to start a group.
2. Who do you think you are? Several months ago, you were not even reading your Bible.
3. Let someone else handle this.

The lies continued. During my Bible reading, I came across Ezra 4:4-5: "Then the peoples around them set out to discourage the people of Judah and make them afraid to go on building. They hired counselors to work against them and frustrate their plans during the entire reign of Cyrus king of Persia and down to the reign of Darius king of Persia."

I was becoming discouraged by the attacks and reached out to whoever I could for support and to help me through the discouragement.

There was a time that I tried to figure this out on my own, but that was just not working, and I asked for the prayers of others. I completely gave the Room of Grace over to the Lord. I was looking forward to the Room of Grace starting, as it was something that I needed in my life as well. On February 11, 2009, the time finally came.

I have never been a numbers guy, but we had twelve people on the first night. I loved having my brother there, as he had been a huge encouragement to me throughout the process of starting the Room of Grace.

Another storm hit in March 2010. I was struggling with my job. I had always worked hard and had been able to produce good numbers for the company that I had worked for previously. The projects that I was working on in my current job were much different than I had been accustomed to, and success was not coming as easily for me as they had in the past. I set the bar too high and was let go. Even though I felt as though I was strong in my reliance on God, the doubts were coming quickly. I was worried. I wanted to quickly find that next forty-hour-a-week job but felt as though God had other plans for me. I had no idea what they were, but I was struggling about what to do. I was so thankful to have both the men at the Tuesday night group as well as the Room of Grace to reach out to for prayer and support. The day that I was let go, I sent an email out asking guys to pray for me. My friend Tim and his father-in-law, both from the Tuesday night group, met me the following morning for breakfast at a small diner. That was a huge moment for me, and I will never forget those two coming to my rescue and reminding me that nothing catches God by surprise.

Because of my involvement with the Room of Grace, I had not been able to make it out to the Tuesday night group as often as I would have liked. I was really struggling with my job loss, and one evening was able to find some time to make the one-hour trip to the meeting. Again, the enemy was feeding me some lies in order to get between me and the relationship that I had developed with the Lord over the last year. A good friend of mine suggested I write down the lies, and if I felt led then I should share them with the group. Below are some of those lies that I shared.

1. I have been faithfully serving the Lord and growing closer to Him, and He, in turn, kicked me where it hurts.
2. I am disqualified from serving the Lord since I cannot hold down a job.
3. I have let my family down.
4. I am not as spiritual as I thought I was.
5. I have lost respect from my peers.
6. I want to give this entire situation over to God, but I do not know how.
7. I can pray, and be encouraged by others, but at the end of the day the result is the same: I am struggling.
8. I can be strong when everything is going well, but I know I am actually weak. So why bother trying to be strong?

Again, these were lies that were being used by the enemy to bring me down. Some of them may not make much sense, but I wrote the lies down as they were being fed to me. Once I opened up and shared the lies with the group, the outpouring of prayers, encouragement, and just overall love from my friends was overwhelming.

One thing that I had wanted to do for awhile now was to start my own business. I had several years of experience in the online marketing field and knew that I had the ability to be on my own. I prayed about it and felt that God was starting to open some doors. Within four weeks of losing my latest job, I started my own business. The Lord was providing.

One of the concerns that Sarah and I had was in the area of health insurance. Since I was going to be self-employed, and Sarah was only working part time, I was going to have to get insurance, and we would have to pay for it ourselves. Sarah and I prayed about it, and within days of us making a decision for me to start my own business, Sarah's employee asked if she would be willing to work full time, thus providing us with full coverage in health insurance. This was such an awesome display of God's provision, and we gave Him all the glory.

The Room of Grace was coming along nicely, and having that night to meet with guys weekly was encouraging.

Our nine-year-old son Gabe is a baseball player and played summer ball. One Saturday afternoon, on May 29, 2010, while at a game of his, my friend Tim from the Tuesday night men's group called. He was distraught. He told me that something terrible had happened. Jon, my friend from the Bulls Tuesday night group, had just taken his own life. This is one of those moments that you really have no clue how to react. Jon had battled with some difficult things in the past, but through the conversations that I had had with him recently, I did not realize that he was currently in a battle strong enough to lead him to taking his life. It was rough the next few days. The funeral was amazing, and I had never been to anything quite like it. There was good music and lots of sharing. Most of the men in our group were there. I left the funeral still in a state of shock and having a hard time believing that Jon was gone. He was very important to me and had been an encouragement to me many times. I have kept a lot of his emails that he sent me and every once in awhile read through some of them.

Soon after the funeral, we dedicated a Tuesday night in honor of Jon. We watched a video clip that consisted of many of his photographs, and a few of us shared how Jon had such a positive influence on our lives as well as on the group as a whole. If you remember, Jon was the warrior of the group, so losing our warrior had a profound effect on us. I know that many of us struggled with his loss, and I was no exception. I had a lot of difficulty handling the situation and entered a dark hole for a couple of weeks. I isolated myself, and that was a bad idea. I wanted to reach out to others in the group but further isolated myself by listening to the excuse that everyone else was struggling as well. Those were some difficult times, and I am thankful that through a lot of prayer, and staying in the Word, I was able to snap out of it. I still miss Jon very much.

Chapter Eight

The Summer of 2010

At the beginning of July 2010, we took a family vacation to a remote area on the west side of Michigan. We spent a great deal of time in research to find a special spot. We rented a home on a bluff with its own private beach. We spent seven nights and eight days there. We arrived on a Saturday and left on the following Saturday. We did so many amazing things during this vacation. We spent an enormous amount of time on the beach. Since it was private, we had a huge area to ourselves and rarely saw anyone.

We had perfect weather the entire week. The only time that it rained was late one evening. We all sat in the living room and watched a huge storm approach us from across Lake Michigan. We should have known that it was going to be a big one since all the ants and other little critters somehow managed to get into the house in hopes that it was a safe haven. The storm was big, but it didn't last for long. Once morning came, the ants had vanished and all that was left was the beautiful calmness of the lake.

One of my favorite parts of the trip was eating dinner on the beach. There was a picnic table sitting directly on the beach, and I loved sitting there, eating with my family with the noise of the waves crashing on the shore.

One day we all went horseback riding. Neither our son Gabe nor our daughter Hope had ever been horseback riding. We reserved the horses and a guide for one hour. Sarah, Gabe, and I had our own horses, while the guide held onto Hope's lead. It was a relaxing and an enjoyable activity to do as a family.

Each evening, after dark, we would roast s'mores over the campfire. We were in such a remote area that there were critters all over the place. After we were inside, we could look out and see the friendly raccoons take whatever we had left behind.

The view from the house was spectacular. Since we were so far up on a bluff, we were overlooking Lake Michigan. Both our living room as well as the master bedroom had huge sliding glass doors. The first thing we would see when we woke up in the morning was the beautiful view of Lake Michigan.

Another day we took a trip to an old lighthouse. For a price, you were able to climb to the top. Once you were at the top, a sign greeted you by stating, "Your shoes are 92 feet up." The view was amazing. We have a lot of pictures depicting our height, and you can easily see in those pictures how windy it was from that high up. I was surprised at how brave the kids were.

My highlight of the trip was when we rented a Jeep Wrangler for a guided tour through the sand dunes. Our guide was amazing and allowed us to freely speed up and down the tall hills. I enjoyed being able to smash the accelerator down as hard as I could. There are a few pictures of me with a smile on my face, and many screams came from our daughter in the back seat. The time at the sand dunes lasted over an hour, right up until dark. If it wasn't so expensive, we would have gladly done it again.

In addition to the highlights above, there were go-kart rides, walks on the beach, driving through beautiful areas with breathtaking views, pier walking, and lots of ice cream. Overall, it was simply a magical time together. On more than one occasion, someone mentioned that this was by far the best family vacation that we had ever had together.

Soon after our summer family vacation, I took a volunteer coaching position for a nine-and-under traveling baseball team. We will be playing in the summer of 2011. Tryouts were held during the summer of 2010, and I am excited about our team and the opportunity to coach my son.

Toward the middle of July 2010, Gabe attended a baseball camp at the University of Michigan. It lasted three days and was very extensive. Gabe and I stayed at a nearby hotel, and we had a great time together. The instruction lasted nearly ten hours a day so, by the time Gabe got back to the hotel, he was exhausted and nearly ready for bed. It was a good time of bonding, and Gabe received some topnotch baseball instruction.

As you can tell, July was a full month. Toward the end of it, we went on a camping trip to Mackinaw City, Michigan, with Sarah's side of the family. We were there for three nights and four days. Our family rented a little cottage that had a view of the Mackinaw Bridge. The cottage had a nice porch, along with one big room with a queen-sized bed, another separate room with bunk beds for the kids, and, most importantly, a bathroom with a shower. Some may call us wimps, but this was my idea of camping. Give me a nice bed, a bathroom, and the ability to gain Internet access, and you can take me nearly anywhere.

The camping trip consisted of relaxing, sitting around campfires, lots of eating, and great fellowship with the family. Our family, along with Sarah's sister and brother-in-law, made a quick trip over the Mackinaw Bridge for a dinner of some incredible-tasting pasties. Everyone was really tired by the end of the four days, but we all had a great time.

July 2010 was an amazing month. It was a month full of family, fun, and relaxation. I cannot remember ever having such a full month of fun.

In August, I received another letter from my church asking if I would consider being on the ballot again for deacon. I hadn't thought about it being this time of year again, but the letter brought back memories of where I was at that point of my life the previous year and how God had been working in my life. This time, I took the decision-making process straight to the Lord and gave it over to Him. The Lord gave me peace, and I accepted the nomination. The voting would be taking place toward the end of the following month.

The last weekend in August, I was asked to be on a softball team that would enter a highly competitive tournament in Battle Creek, Michigan. I had been playing ball all summer and was excited to go away for the weekend and play. I stayed at a hotel near the softball complex along with a couple of guys in the tournament that I knew. The weather was nice, but it was really hot this particular weekend. We won a couple of games and did fairly well for the level of competition that was there, but we did not place anywhere near the top tier. Throughout the tournament, I noticed that I would get tired more easily than normal, and I also dealt with some shortness-of-breath issues. I assumed that it was the heat but was surprised as I had been riding my bike daily all summer without any issues.

Chapter Nine

"Call 911"

My brothers-in-law and I planned another bike trip for October 9–10. We had had a great time last year and decided to go ahead and do it again. This time we were going to go from Midland to Clare, Michigan. Overall, it would be about an eighty-mile round trip. There is a really nice trail that goes nearly the entire route, and we reserved a nice little cabin in Clare to rest and spend the night on Saturday the ninth. I had been consistently riding my bike fifteen to twenty miles a day several days a week. At thirty-eight years old, I was the eldest of the four of us, so I felt that it was necessary for me to train as much as possible in order to keep up with the younger guys. The bike that I was currently riding was a mountain bike. I enjoyed road biking much more and had put some road compatible tires on my mountain bike. I have always dreamed of getting a new road bike and after a lot of research purchased a TREK Madone 5.1. I purchased the new bike just a couple weeks before our bike trip and wanted to get better acquainted with my new bike, so I was riding it every day.

As October 2010 began, I felt as though I was getting a cold. I was hoping that it was not bronchitis as I tend to get bronchitis yearly but usually not until later into winter. By October 5, I was not feeling well at all. My chest was achy, and I was starting to get body aches. On Wednesday,

October 6, I decided to call the doctors and make an appointment. I was scheduled for Thursday, October 7, at 9:45 a.m. to see my family doctor.

By the time Thursday morning rolled around, I was feeling really crummy. I had body aches, my chest was tight, and I had some discomfort in my jaw. I was starting to assume that I had a nasty cold, flu, or virus of some sort. My doctor was not in that day, so I saw the nurse practitioner. She looked in my ears, nose, and throat and listened to my chest and lungs. Everything seemed to be routine up to this point. She asked me if I knew about my heart murmur. I told her that, approximately six months ago, I had gone into the emergency room because of a horrible cough in which I had started coughing up a little blood. While in the emergency room, the doctor had made a similar comment. The doctor at that time asked me the same question, and I told her that no one had ever told me about a murmur. She said that although the murmur was faint, she could definitely hear it. The nurse practitioner said that this one wasn't faint, and she could hear it very well. She did not appear overly concerned and said that it did appear that I had a virus that had been going around. My symptoms were very similar to others that had this particular virus. However, she ordered an EKG while I was there in the office and said that they were going to schedule me for an echocardiogram for a later date. Once the echocardiogram was scheduled, I would be informed of the appointment time.

Several minutes later, another nurse entered the room, hooked me up to all the wires, and administered the EKG test. Once the test was finished, the nurse said that she didn't think that she received a good reading and ran another EKG test. Once I was finished, I went home and back to work.

I could not get the brothers-in-law bike trip off my mind. I knew it was coming in two days and I could not wait to go. Up until just recently, I was feeling really well, had been training consistently, and had a brand new bike. The trip was all planned out. One of my brothers-in-law was coming from Cleveland, Ohio, along with his wife Amanda.

By the time late afternoon on Thursday rolled around, I was taking a turn for the worse. I was really achy, had a little shortness of breath, and was really tired. Rather than risking having to cancel the day before or the day of the bike trip, I contacted my brother-in-law who was going to be coming in from Grand Rapids, Michigan, and let him know that I had to cancel. I told him that I felt really badly, but I was afraid of getting part way into the trip and becoming sicker. I had this fear that I may be coming down with the flu, and riding a bike for over forty miles in one day is not a place that you would want to be while fighting an illness. My brother-in-law indicated that he may contact the other two and cancel the trip. I told him that I really did not want them to cancel for my sake, and that they should go on ahead without me. There was a part of me that was still hoping that I would miraculously get better over the course of the next twenty-four hours and still be able to go on the trip. However, by the time Thursday evening rolled around, I knew that I was not going to be able to go anywhere in my condition. Although I was getting really ill, I was considerably disappointed that this had happened the day before the big bike trip.

At around 5:00 p.m. on Thursday, I dropped Gabe off at football practice, which was a quarter of a mile from our house. Normally I would stay and watch, but, since I was sick, I came home for a little while. I went back to football practice and watched Gabe for a few minutes before his practice was over. Gabe and I came home, ate supper, and relaxed for the rest of the evening. Gabe and Hope went to bed at their normal time, which was around 8:30 p.m. Sarah and I hung out for the rest of the evening and watched a little television.

At approximately 11:30 p.m., we went up to bed. By this time, my jaw was pounding and my chest ached. After we got into bed, I tried to lie down, but when I rested my head on the pillow, the intensity of my jaw pounding increased. I sat a couple of pillows upright to see if that would help. I was really tired by this time and just wanted to fall asleep. Unfortunately, the pounding in my jaw would not allow me to even begin to think about sleeping.

I decided to get back up and go into the basement to watch some television. Soon after I was settled into the couch and had the television on, the intensity of the pounding in both my chest and jaw increased. My chest and jaw pounded so hard and so quickly that it was like someone had flipped a switch from low to high. The pain and the fierceness of the pounding caught me by surprise. I had been uncomfortable for over three days, so I wasn't expected anything to come on so quickly like this. I remember standing up and doubling over a little bit to see if that would relieve the pain. As I looked at the clock, I noticed that it was a little after midnight.

The pain only got worse, and I was starting to feel dizzy. I have tried hard to remember all the thoughts that were going through my head at this moment. As strange as it may sound, the thought of a heart attack never entered into my mind. When I talk to people about this moment, the first thing they ask me is whether or not I thought I was having a heart attack. The only explanation that I can give is that my mind was working on overdrive to get myself up two flights of stairs and back into our bedroom to where Sarah was sleeping.

I started the climb from the basement up the first flight of stairs into the kitchen. I was doubled over a little bit with one hand clinching my chest and the other hand balancing myself on each step. Once I made it up these stairs and into the kitchen, I stopped for a couple moments to collect myself. I made my way down the short hallway to the next flight of stairs. I have had some people ask me why I didn't yell at this point. I have a couple explanations that might help explain my thought process. The first explanation is that while I was stepping up onto the first step on the second flight of stairs leading up to the play room area, I knew that Gabe and Hope would be sound asleep. They had school in the morning and I did not want to wake them or get them concerned. The second reason was the same as the reason I gave earlier. I was focused on getting to the bedroom.

I continued up the second flight of stairs into the upper level of the house and into the playroom area. I again stopped for a couple of minutes once I reached the top in order to catch my breath. I then proceeded down the short hallway that led to our bedroom. I reached out with one hand and slowly opened the door. What humors me, as I think back on it now, is that by force of habit I was slowly opening the door in order not to disturb Sarah, who was sleeping and had to work in the morning. So here I was, desperate to get two flights up the stairs to Sarah, and I was mentally thinking of how I needed to be careful not to disturb her.

Sarah has a sixth sense for people in trouble. After I opened the door, but did not turn on the light, I whispered Sarah's name. She hopped out of bed and exclaimed, *"What's wrong?"*

I reached over and turned the light on while still clinching my chest and doubling over with the other hand. I told Sarah that the pains in my chest and jaw were excruciating. Sarah had known that I was having some pains when I left to go to the basement. She immediately got dressed and asked if I wanted her to call 911. The obvious answer as to whether or not I needed 911 called was *yes*. I am sure others have been in the position before when, just at the moment that 911 is about to be called, you have that small moment of doubt. You ask yourself whether or not you're overreacting. I was thinking the same thing to myself while at the same time clinching my chest in pain. I told Sarah to wait just a minute. I don't think a full minute passed and the pounding was getting so severe that I told her that I was in trouble. I said, "Call 911."

Looking back at the pain that I was in, I am surprised that I was able to get up the stairs and dressed. I put a different t-shirt on along with some sweatpants and socks. Sarah and I then went back down one flight of stairs into the kitchen. We managed to stay quiet enough not to disturb Gabe and Hope. I had a seat on a stool at the counter and waited for the ambulance to arrive.

A paramedic arrived first at our house rather quickly. He came through the front door, and, as he approached me, he asked me to explain what was going on. I walked him through everything that had happened up to this point. The paramedic then started to hook me up to a portable EKG monitor. When the paramedic was about finished hooking me up, the ambulance arrived. There were two men in the ambulance. The paramedic and the two ambulance drivers obviously knew each other as they exchanged pleasantries.

I told the paramedic that I had had an EKG the morning before and that it did not show anything abnormal. The paramedic quickly explained, in those quick medical terms, to the ambulance guys what my chief complaint was. As the EKG was running, he asked whether or not I had had any heart or temporomandibular joint disorder related issues in the past. About the same time that I was answering the paramedics question with a hearty, "No," Sarah suggested that I had had temporomandibular joint disorder. Once I was finished glaring at her with that *Don't give them any reason not to check everything out* stare, I explained that my jaw would occasionally click, but I had never been diagnosed with TMJ.

As I was speaking to the paramedic, the ambulance driver had brought the gurney to the front door and asked if I could walk to it. I got up and walked to the gurney, and they proceeded to load and strap me onto it. The ambulance drivers then pushed me into the cold night air, down our steep driveway, and into the waiting ambulance, which was located at the end of our driveway. While I was being loaded into the ambulance, Sarah was inside the house making a phone call to her mom asking if she could come over and watch Gabe and Hope. Sarah's mom lives about fifteen minutes away, so she would be able to get there quickly.

Once I was settled inside the ambulance, I was hooked up to a more extensive EKG monitor. Another test was run, but they did not find anything out of the ordinary. Once the EKG test was completed, my finger was pricked in order to see the level of my blood sugar, which checked out fine as well. After my blood sugar was checked, I was hooked up to a heart monitor and blood pressure cuff. Up to this point, I had not been administered any medications, and surprisingly my pain had not gotten any worse. I was asked what hospital I wanted to be taken to, and I indicated that I wanted to go to Genesys, which was about a twenty-minute drive. I knew that the EKG had checked out fine, and that there was nothing unusual showing on my heart monitor. I was starting to wonder if I did truly have a virus or the flu. I asked if it was possible to skip going to the hospital altogether. The paramedic told me that they would never recommend skipping a trip to the hospital. He said that we should always assume that if I was ill enough to call an ambulance, then I should always go to the hospital regardless.

The doors were closed and at approximately 12:45 a.m. we were on our way to the hospital.

While on our way, I was given a nitroglycerin pill and an aspirin. I was warned that the nitroglycerin pill may give me a headache, and it did not take long for that to prove true. The nitroglycerin pill worked quickly, and the pounding in my chest and jaw subsided significantly. I was given a second nitroglycerin pill a few minutes later.

We arrived at the hospital within twenty minutes, and I was unloaded and checked in. Initially the action was fast and furious. As soon as I arrived, I was hooked up to their monitors, received a blood-pressure check, and had an IV placed in my arm.

I remember that I had a feeling that I might be going through an awful lot for nothing. By this time, I did not have a significant amount of pain, and the virus that I heard about earlier started to sound like it may be the culprit. I was convinced that if I was having a heart attack, then the EKG wouldn't look so normal, and my pain would not be getting better.

A D-dimer test was taken to rule out any possible pulmonary embolisms. The D-dimer test came back a little high, and, based off some of my symptoms, one of the doctors on duty requested a CAT scan. The request for this test proved to be one of the decisions that saved my life. I had never had a CAT scan before. I was wheeled, while on my bed, to a room that had a huge cylinder-looking machine. I was moved from my bed onto a bed that was connected to the cylinder. One of the persons that administered the CAT scan hooked a line up to my IV. It was explained to me that I would be asked to hold my breath and would go in and out of the machine. A dye substance would be sent into my body and would feel very warm. I must say that when the dye squirted throughout my body, I was not prepared for the sensation that would follow. There was no pain, but it was not a comfortable test.

After the test was over, I was moved back onto my original bed and wheeled back into my room. I was hooked back up to the monitors and blood cuff and settled in until we heard the results of the CAT scan.

Chapter Ten

The Diagnosis

At about 4:30 a.m., while Sarah was nestled into an uncomfortable chair and I was gazing up into the ceiling, one of the doctors entered the room. The expression on his face is something that is burned into my mind. I could tell that the news that he was about to give me was serious. The doctor came up to my bed, and said, "The good news is that you are still here with us."

At this moment, my heart sank. The first thought that came into my mind was that I was going to be told that they found a mass of some sort, and that I had cancer. The doctor proceeded to tell me that the CAT scan had shown an aneurysm on my aorta that was causing my aorta to dissect. At this moment, I was starting to get very warm and flush. The doctor said that the situation could turn catastrophic very quickly. He explained that a surgery team was being prepared, and that my heart rate would have to immediately be lowered in preparation for the surgery.

An aortic dissection is when the inner wall of the aorta tears. Once the tear happens, blood will flow between the walls of the aorta and continue to force the layers apart. Mine was a type A and Type B dissection. This means that my tear was in the arch area of the aorta near the heart and had moved farther down the aorta.

I didn't grasp right away that the surgery the doctor was referring to was open heart. I remember asking the doctor if the surgery was open heart surgery, and he confirmed it.

At this moment, the doctor walked out, and there was a very short moment where Sarah and I were in the room alone. I looked over at Sarah, who probably had nearly the same expression on her face that I did, and I remember shrugging my shoulders and just looked at her. There was a moment where I truly did not have any idea what to say. Being speechless was an understatement. It was approximately 5:00 a.m.

I could tell by the expression on the doctors' faces that they were surprised that I was lying there talking to them after knowing what I was suffering from.

Based on the circumstances in front of me, I knew that I was not going to make it. I had a feeling that, on this day, I was going to die. I looked over at Sarah and said, "I am ready to see Christ." Even though I was thinking this, I am still surprised that the words left my mouth. When later speaking to Sarah about this moment, she said that, as she was looking back at me, she remembers thinking that she didn't even know what song I wanted played at my funeral.

The doctors and nurses came back in and started to prepare me for surgery. I asked Sarah for my cell phone so that I could give my brother a call and let him know what was happening. When my brother answered the phone I said to him, "I am in the emergency room in Genesys. I am going to have open-heart surgery. You know what to do." I knew that is all I had to tell him in order for him to make the right calls in order to get people praying. I sent a text to another friend as well. By this time, there was a lot going on around me.

Sarah wanted her mom at the hospital with her, so she called her mom who was staying at our house while the kids were sleeping. Sarah's mom called Sarah's sister Lydia to go to our house and watch the kids.

By this time, there were some medications that were being administered to me, and this is where my memory cut off. I don't remember a thing beyond this point, even though I was conscious up to the time of the surgery. Sarah and I have spoken in length and detail about the amazing display of prayer and the love shown by many people during my surgery.

My brother-in-law had contacted our pastor who arrived at the hospital at around 6:00 a.m. The pastor read a passage from Philippians and prayed with us. Even though I don't remember this, Sarah has mentioned several times how much comfort our pastor provided.

Not too long after we were told that everything was being prepared for surgery, we were informed that there was a change of plans. The surgeon wanted to give me the best chance possible to spare my aortic valve. Genesys does not do valve-sparing surgeries, so he wanted to send me to the University of Michigan hospital in Ann Arbor. The surgeon was going to check if a surgery team was available there and also make sure a helicopter was available to fly me to Ann Arbor. A short time later, we were informed that everything was all set and a helicopter from the University of Michigan hospital was on its way to get me.

A friend of Sarah's, Kim, tells another story about how God was placing people around me to provide a much needed prayer chain. Kim's boss was in Genesys at the time and was in an emergency room directly across the hall from us. He saw all the commotion, including the life flight team that came and transported me. Kim visited her boss Saturday morning at the hospital and explained that she was going to Ann Arbor to be with a friend whose husband had gone through surgery the previous day. Kim told her boss that I had been at Genesys the previous morning and was airlifted to Ann Arbor because of an aortic dissection. Her boss was able to describe both Sarah and me, and told Kim that he had prayed for us. I believe God was strategically placing people in positions to pray.

When I received the news that I would be going into surgery, my mom was out of town, about three hours north, with some relatives. Sarah called her cell phone and my mom's phone happened to be by her bed so she was able to hear it vibrate. She answered the call. This is another instance when God was working to get more people praying. My mom got everyone together and they immediately started praying for me. They started their drive back so that my mom could be there for me. My mom's aunt was in the car and she had a son who was a doctor. They called him and explained what was happening to me. He was very honest in telling my mom that there was a really good possibility that I was not going to make it. This obviously was not what my mom needed or wanted to hear, but it was an honest assessment of the situation. My mom tells how difficult it was to be in a car, and go through a three-hour trip, when she knew the severity of what was happening to me.

By this time, Sarah's mom, our pastor, my brother Tim, and his in-laws were all at the hospital. A lot had happened in an hour and a half, and at 6:30 a.m. the flight crew from Ann Arbor had arrived. Emergency personnel were preparing me for my flight to the University of Michigan hospital. Once I left, all of the people who were at Genesys made their way to Ann Arbor, which was about a forty-five-minute drive.

At approximately 7:00 a.m., I arrived at the U of M hospital, and was taken to their emergency room in order to prepare me for surgery. Sarah and everyone else arrived a little over a half hour later. Sarah had assumed that they would be taking me back to surgery the moment that I arrived, so she was both surprised and happy when they told her that she could come back and be with me until the surgery.

The emergency room staff allowed two people at a time to see me. Sarah and my brother came first, and then others followed. Once everyone had come to see me, Sarah and my brother came in to be with me. The nurse that was taking care of me explained in more detail what questions the surgeon would ask once he arrived. Sarah told me that I asked the nurse a question about how long my recovery was going to take. The nurse gave a *That is something we don't need to worry about right now expression*. I assume that she was thinking more about how I was going to survive than about how long my recovery would take.

Shortly thereafter, my surgeon arrived. Dr. Patel explained the risks involved with the surgery that I would be undergoing. In addition to death, the risks included stroke and kidney failure.

If you remember, the main reason that we were sent to the University of Michigan hospital was to save my valve. The surgeon, after seeing the CAT scan that was taken at Genesys, indicated that it was not going to be possible to spare my valve. Because of the inability to spare my valve, I had to choose between a mechanical and a tissue/pig valve. The differences between these two valves were explained to us. A mechanical valve can last a lifetime, and an additional surgery to replace this valve is typically not needed. I would have to take blood thinner medication and would have to be careful with my activities. With a tissue valve, I would be able to participate in more extreme sports. However, a tissue valve typically lasts between ten and fifteen years, and I would have to eventually go through another open heart surgery.

While the information was being explained to me, I was fading in and out, and the surgeon had to continually keep me alert in order to provide me with the information. After everything was explained to me, I chose the mechanical valve and signed the consent forms. To this day, as I explained earlier, I have no memory of anything that took place from 5:00 a.m. at the emergency room at Genesys.

Just prior to leaving for surgery, all of my loved ones at the hospital were called into my room. My brother called my mom, who was still on her way home from being out of town, and put me on the phone to speak to her. My mom said that I told her that I loved her. After I spoke to my mom, my brother prayed.

It was also during this time that Sarah and I discussed whether or not we wanted to call Gabe and Hope so that I could speak to them before going into surgery. Again, I have no memory of this conversation, but

Sarah explained that it was a difficult decision. We knew there was a really good chance that I was not going to live, yet we did not want to worry the kids. I know that Gabe particularly would have sensed the severity of the situation and would have worried immensely. We decided not to call the kids. It is hard to know whether or not we made the right decision, but as I look back at everything, I realize that God was in control.

Everyone was able to follow me right up to the point where I entered the surgery area. As I was being led down the hallway to the surgery unit, one of the anesthesiologists told Sarah that I was in good hands. The anesthesiologist stated that they did nearly fifty of these types of surgeries a year. Sarah has said that knowing this provided some comfort, and she was thankful that God had cleared the path for me to be at the University of Michigan hospital.

A good friend of mine from the Tuesday night men's group called my cell phone just as I was about to leave everyone for the surgery. Sarah answered the phone and was able to talk to him. He let us know that he was praying for us, and Sarah was able to share that with me at the last moment.

Chapter Eleven

Surgery

At approximately 8:30 a.m., I was taken into surgery. Sarah and everyone else who was there were taken into the ICU waiting room. There were only a few other people in the waiting room, and Sarah later found out that surgeries were not normally conducted on Fridays. Again, God was taking care of me by making a surgery team available.

Sarah updated her status on Facebook at 8:59 a.m. on October 8 and it read, "Please pray for my husband Walt. He is about to go into emergency surgery at U of M for a dissected aorta. This is a life threatening surgery." There were dozens of replies in a show of support and indications of prayer. I go back and read these often as a reminder of everyone that God sent into our life on that day as support.

From this time forward, there was an overwhelming outpouring of support. I would have to say that this is one of the most difficult parts of this journey to fully grasp. The prayer chain that developed was amazing. The links of the prayer chain kept connecting and growing.

At approximately 9:30 a.m., someone came into the waiting room and informed everyone that my chest had been opened. We were told that the surgery would last a minimum of eight to ten hours.

Sarah did an amazing job keeping people informed on Facebook, and we have been told by many that it was appreciated. She updated her status reports and wrote notes that allowed people to pray more specifically. This is one area that is just really hard to emphasize. The amount of people that were reaching out overwhelms me to this day. I look back at the Facebook messages that were pouring in and see how great God's power was displayed through so many people. There were people sending messages of support that we did not even know. I had friends from my Facebook page from other states and they were sharing with me how they had their church members praying. Social networking can sometimes be a sinkhole of time, but in this case God used the technology that is available in this day and age to spread the word about my condition, which enabled people to pray more specifically for me.

The news of my surgery spread as far as Australia with people praying. I could continue to go on, but I cannot properly express how much God was holding me and my family up through the prayers of so many. There were so many blessings being showered on us. Had I not undergone heart surgery, I would never have been the recipient of all the amazing blessings God showered on my life through the power of prayer and the friends and family. He sent all of this into my life to encourage me and meet my needs.

God was also working out the details of my business as well. Sarah was able to make contact with my clients and informed them about my condition. I am so thankful for how supportive my clients were.

Throughout the day, family and friends arrived at the hospital and provided support for Sarah. She tells a story of how over a dozen people placed their chairs in a circle, and anyone who wanted to would randomly pray. I feel so blessed to have had so much support from so many people, and I also am thankful that God provided that support group for Sarah.

There is a song that was constantly on Sarah's mind, and provided her with much needed comfort. The song and parts of the lyrics are based on

Romans 8:31, which says, "What, then, shall we say in response to these things? If God is for us, who can be against us?"

There were so many emotions that took place for Sarah during this day, and she continued to get bombarded with calls, text messages, and Facebook messages. It was as though God was showering Sarah with his love through other people. Each time that someone new arrived in the waiting room, it would prove to be a huge comfort for Sarah.

Sarah shared with me a conversation she had with her friend Megan. Megan is married to my friend Tim who nearly died of meningitis. She knew what it was like to be in a situation where her husband may not make it and provided a level of comfort that was very much needed at that time. We know that circumstances such as these, and the people that God led to the waiting room at precisely the right time, were not random events.

We have heard of stories in which someone lost a loved one. The person who suffered the loss would tell how he or she had just done something really special with his or her loved one and was happy for that opportunity before the loved one passed away. Sarah shared with her friend that, since we had had a great summer together, especially the family vacation we had taken not too long ago, maybe this was going to be that situation. Maybe she was going to look back and be able to remember the fond moments we had as a family just before my passing. This is a glimpse into some of the emotions that Sarah was dealing with at the time.

In addition to the many different levels of emotions that went on during the surgery, there were times of laughter between the times of distress. When I had heard that there were actually people laughing at times while I was in surgery, my first thought was, "Wait a minute, how could anyone be laughing while I was barely clinging to life?" I am reminded that God can use different emotions to provide comfort and am thankful for the people who were with Sarah and were able to provide humor at times in order to lighten the mood. It is hard for me to fully understand the roller coaster ride of emotions that my family and friends had to endure that day.

Sarah shared how guilty she felt for crying so much, as she thought that it showed her lack of trust toward God. I know that one of the things that God did for us during this trial was to build our faith and trust in Him. We realize that trusting God isn't just about trusting that everything will turn out as perfectly as we think it should, but that we can trust God to help us through the circumstance, from beginning to end, no matter what the result turns out to be. The result may not always be the result that we desire, but if we give our trust over to the Lord, He will guide us through it.

There were many times that Sarah thought about Gabe and Hope. She would wonder how they would handle not having a father. I have a special relationship with both of my children, but we know that Gabe would particularly have a tough time dealing with everything if I did not make it. There are many times that I look back and thank the Lord for sparing me for my children's sake and for allowing me to continue living and being with them.

Sarah was also thinking about how thankful she was that God provided her with a full-time job with excellent health insurance. We considered it a huge answer to prayer when Sarah got the job, but we believe that God was taking care of us back then for this particular trial.

Back at home, Sarah's sister and brother-in-law were taking care of Gabe and Hope. Sarah wanted to call and see how they were doing but was afraid that she would be too emotional and worry the kids. When she called them, God provided her with the strength she needed to get through the phone call without breaking down. Gabe and Hope were doing fine, and Lydia had taken them to the school's homecoming. Many people had heard that I was in surgery and were coming up to the kids, letting them know that they were praying for me. God was showing my kids how He was taking care of me.

After the initial update at 9:30 a.m., not many updates were provided. My family was hoping that *no news must be good news.*

Once Sarah knew that I was more than eight hours into my surgery, she knew that the time was close to everything being put back together and turned back on. She knew that this was a critical part of the surgery and was praying that everything would work properly.

My brother tells a great story that involves him and our grandpa. As I mentioned earlier in my story, my grandma, who meant a lot to us, passed away in January 2009. That part of my story shares how God used the circumstances surrounding my grandma's death to bring us into a closer relationship with Christ. My grandma's name was Evelyn.

When it got later in the day, the person at the desk in the ICU waiting room let everyone know that he was leaving. If they had any questions, they could speak to a lady who was located through a set of doors and within the surgery area. That person's name, they were told, was Evelyn.

A while later, my brother and Grandpa were on a walk. My grandpa was getting antsy to hear some news about how the surgery was going and told my brother that he would like to ask Evelyn if there were any updates about my progress. My brother, who had not heard the announcement of the person's name being Evelyn, thought my grandpa was losing his mind and was referring to my deceased grandma. Once it was figured out who my grandpa was actually referring to, everyone got a good chuckle out of it. I don't believe that the name being the same was random. I would like to think that there was an angel sent to watch over both me and my family.

Chapter Twelve

Out of Surgery

At 8:20 p.m., on Friday, October 8, 2010, after nearly eleven hours of surgery, Dr. Patel entered the waiting room. Sarah could tell by Dr. Patel's demeanor that the news was possibly good.

At the time that my surgery ended, there were about fifteen people in the waiting room supporting us. When Dr. Patel walked toward the group, everyone circled around him in anticipation of the news. He explained that everything went as well as it could have under the circumstances. A piece of really good news was that they were able to save my valve. This was such an answer to prayer. I didn't have to receive the mechanical valve, which meant that I would not have to be on blood thinner. Dr. Patel went on to explain that I was on the heart and lung machine for twenty-nine minutes. Forty minutes is considered the maximum time that someone can be on the machine. The portion of damaged area in the arch of my aorta was removed and replaced with a Dacron graft.

It was explained that the next twenty-four hours would be critical for how my organs would respond, and I was not out of the woods yet. I needed to be monitored for a little while longer and then would be taken to recovery. Once I was in recovery, people could start coming back and seeing me.

Once Dr. Patel left, my grandpa prayed with everyone, thanking God for bringing me through the surgery.

I love hearing what my grandpa had to say about the moment that Dr. Patel was informing everyone about the results of the surgery. My grandpa is very hard of hearing and could not hear anything that Dr. Patel was saying. He looked around at everyone's expressions and could tell that it was good news. Of course, later he got a full report.

Below is a Facebook note that Sarah wrote twelve minutes after the surgeon gave everyone the news. Sometimes we don't think about how encouraging it is to look back and see the rawness of a message that was left. I get emotional each time I see this message from Sarah.

Walt Conger update - out of surgery
by Sarah Conger on Friday, October 8, 2010, at 8:32 p.m.

Just to let you know Walt is out of surgery. The doctor came out around 8:20. The surgery went as smooth as possible and they were able to save his valve, which is a huge blessing since he will not need blood thinner! They will watch him for a few more minutes and then keep him asleep tonight. They will be monitoring him for any organ damage or any other effects. Please continue to pray as he is not out of the woods yet as these next hours are crucial. God is good. Thanks for all your prayers and messages.

Soon after I was moved into the recovery room, some of the people that were still at the hospital came back to see me. Sarah was warned that my color might be a lot different, and that I could be very bloated. Once they entered my room, Sarah was surprised as to how good I actually looked. She was also surprised that my color did not look any different from normal. I was a little bloated, but not as much as she had expected. Sarah was expecting the worst and was pleasantly surprised. She described, in detail, how encouraged she was when she saw my chest moving up and down.

Arrangements were made for Sarah, my mom, and my brother to spend the night at the hospital's hotel. They rested as much as they could and were back to see me early the next morning.

It was Saturday, October 9, 2010. I was going to remain heavily sedated in order to allow me to get the rest that I needed and also to help me better tolerate the breathing tube. As soon as Sarah arrived on Saturday morning, she came into my room to see me. I was having a rough time with the breathing tube and was choking on it. Seeing me struggle with the breathing tube was very difficult for her. After a few minutes, Sarah decided to take a little walk.

My vital signs were stable, and I was continuing to improve. Since everything was looking good, by the time that Sarah came back from her walk my breathing tube had been removed.

Below is Sarah's Facebook message for Saturday, October 9, 2010.

Walt Conger Update - Saturday 10/9
by Sarah Conger on Saturday, October 9, 2010, at 9:18 p.m.

Thank you everyone for your prayers. Walt is progressing well today. The breathing tube is out, all his vitals are good, and his kidneys are working properly. He is drinking water and starting to be more coherent. We are excited about his progress and it is truly a miracle from God that he is alive today. Thanks so much for your love and support! There are so many amazing stories of people praying and I can't wait to share them with Walt when he is better.

It was a nice clear day and it was also the day of the big Michigan versus Michigan State football game. I received several visitors off and on throughout Saturday, and spent nearly the entire day sleeping. Around dinner time, Sarah had gone to get something to eat. My brother and mom were in the room with me. I opened my eyes and asked what had happened. My mom explained the best that she could what had happened. My mom notified Sarah and she returned to see me. Unfortunately, I still have no memories of this day. I realize that it is probably for my own good, but it can be frustrating at times to lose so many days from my memory.

Sarah's brother Jon and sister-in-law Amanda from Cleveland, Ohio, arrived on Saturday. Amanda told Sarah that she wanted to help out in any way that she could, and both Jon and Amanda stayed overnight at the hotel with Sarah.

Sunday was the big day for me. Up to this point, as I explained earlier, I had no memory since 5:00 a.m. on Friday, October 8. At around 10:30 a.m. on Sunday, October 10, the first thing I remember was hearing a nurse instruct me to take a deep breath in and then let it out. I wish I could properly describe this moment. It was as if I was under water coming toward the surface and then dramatically broke the plane of the surface and everything came into focus.

As I let my breath out, the nurse removed my chest tubes. I remember the sensation being very uncomfortable. I then heard the demands repeated. I took another deep breath in and then let it out. This time, the nurse removed my catheter. The catheter being removed was by far one of the most painful experiences I have ever encountered. This was the moment that I returned to the world, and my post-surgery memory begins.

The next several hours were a whirlwind of emotions for me. If you recall, one of the last moments that I remember is realizing that I was not going to make it through this. Waking up and coming back into reality was surprising to me. I assumed that I was going to die, and now I was waking up, flat on my back and seeing Sarah for the first time.

I can remember everything from this moment forward, yet it was hard for me to fully grasp what had happened. I knew that I had had major surgery, but I did not understand quite yet what was going on around me. I didn't realize the severity of what took place, or the support that was going on around me. I could tell by the faces of everyone who was coming to see me that what had happened was a miracle.

Walt Conger Update - 10/10 Sunday Morning
by Sarah Conger on Sunday, October 10, 2010, at 10:02 a.m.

Walt was sitting up in his chair when we went in to see him this morning. He looks good and ate some Jell-O. He asked me a lot of questions about what happened and I think he is trying to put this all together in his mind but is too tired to think. His white blood count is slightly elevated this morning so they've removed any extra IVs. Please pray no infection sets in and he can continue to improve. The nurse told me they will be taking him for a walk shortly. Thanks again for your prayers. God is good and He gives us more than we can ask or think.

I remember seeing and being able to hear what Sarah was telling me, although everything was foggy. One of the first things I remember her saying was that one of my favorite authors had left a message on my Facebook page saying that he was praying for me. I later realized this author has thousands of followers on his Facebook page. By him leaving me a one-sentence message, it linked to an enormous prayer chain. This was another situation where God was taking care of me.

There were a handful of visitors on Sunday. I was not very coherent for a good portion of the day but did recognize people and was encouraged by their visits. As the day went on, I began to develop an appetite and felt like I was able to understand what was going on a bit better. I was very uncomfortable when it came time to walk. I felt very insecure standing up and walked about a hundred feet my first time. I could not wait to get back to my room and chair. I continued to be resistant to the goals that were placed before me, but thankfully I had nurses who were persistent. Later in the day, a couple of physical therapists stopped by and took me for a longer walk. I was still uncomfortable but did a little better during my second walk of the day.

Sunday continued to be a strange day for me. As I mentioned before, this was the first day that I started remembering, but it was a day that mostly consisted of trying to get a grip on what I had been through, and what was going to happen going forward.

Sarah went home on Sunday night to get some things that she needed and to see the kids. She had not been home for a couple of days. Amanda stayed at our house and took care of the kids during the rest of my stay in the hospital. Amanda was an absolute blessing. She did so much for us and went above and beyond. Having her stay at our house and with the kids allowed us a much needed peace of mind. Because of Amanda's willingness to stay at our house, Gabe and Hope were able to go about their normal routine, which included school, homework, practices, etc. We will never forget the sacrifices that she made for us.

It was awesome to see God take care of so many of the details from the very beginning. On October 8, Sarah's mom was available to come directly to our house in order to stay with the kids. Later that night, Sarah's sister Lydia was available to come over and allow Sarah's mom to go to the hospital in time to drive with Sarah to Ann Arbor. God's handling of the details continued, and I am thankful for the display of God's care.

On Monday, I continued to make progress. I was able to move around a little bit more and took a couple of longer walks. At approximately 5:00 p.m., I was moved out of ICU and to a regular room in the cardiac unit. Sarah and I remember how strange it was to leave the security of the ICU and the constant personal care of the nurses and move into a new environment with new nurses and other tenants. It was a relief to have the wires to my IVs removed. Going from the ICU to this new room felt like

Out of Surgery

being a battery unhooked from a charger. The time between the world coming back into focus for me and being moved out of ICU seemed to happen very quickly. It had only been seventy-two hours since my surgery had concluded, and I was already out of the ICU. My only explanation for this would be the power of prayer.

The room was set up a lot different from what I had seen before. Instead of one big room with the beds side by side, only separated by a curtain, it was one huge room with the beds lined up long ways with a wall between each section. This setup provided some sense of privacy. By the time I settled into my new room, it was getting late, and I was extremely tired from a day spent communicating and walking more. Sarah left for home in the evening and would be back early the next morning.

Sleep was very hard to come by on Monday night. I was very tired but was too uncomfortable to sleep. I watched a little bit of Monday Night Football until my eyes got too heavy to keep open. I had to sit upright because of my sternum and could never get comfortable. It was frustrating simply going to the bathroom. I was in so much discomfort and still very weak; just getting out of bed and to the bathroom was a chore. By the time Tuesday morning rolled around, I was tired, frustrated, needed to brush my teeth, and needed to clean up. I felt dirty and grimy. I wanted Sarah badly and was getting impatient.

At approximately 9:45 a.m., Sarah arrived, and I can remember clearly how relieved I was to see her. She was able to get all the toiletries that I needed. She also brought some clothes for me to change into. I was looking forward to getting out of my hospital gown and into shorts and a t-shirt. Sarah and I went into the bathroom, and I was able to brush my teeth and clean myself up while dodging the many heart-monitor wires that were attached to me. Once I was cleaned and dressed, I made my way into my chair and was feeling a little bit better. It was discouraging that a simple chore such as washing up and brushing my teeth was so difficult to do. I kept hearing people telling me to give it time, but these were not the words that were ringing through my mind as I was moaning in pain from simply bending over the sink.

Tuesday was a relaxing day. Sarah and I were alone for a good portion of the day and were able to talk. I asked a lot of questions and got some additional clarity on all that took place. This was the first day that I was able to get a hold of my cell phone. I was overwhelmed by all the emails, text messages, and Facebook messages that were on my phone. There were literally hundreds. It was very emotional reading through the messages and seeing firsthand all the prayer support that I was receiving. Sarah and I had spoken about how much it meant to us to be receiving so much support. A person may have a good idea about the friends that he or she has, but until that person goes through a tragedy such as what I went through, and gets to see the support in action, he or she just doesn't truly know to what degree that support is. I wish that I could thank everyone face to face who contacted me through this trial, or prayed for me. I know that is impossible, but it meant that much to my family and me.

Dr. Patel visited on Tuesday morning, and we received a little more insight to what had happened. I had an aortic aneurysm that caused the aorta to dissect. There is still a tear in the upper part of the aorta, but Dr. Patel felt as though he fixed everything that needed to be fixed at the time. I will have to have yearly visits to keep a watchful eye on this tear. If the tear gets worse, I will have to have an additional surgery. I was reminded how God protected me. Very few people survive an aorta dissection, and of those who make it to the operating room, one in four never go home.

Walt Conger Improvement Update - Tuesday Oct. 12
by Sarah Conger on Tuesday, October 12, 2010, at 3:12 p.m.

I wanted to let everyone know that Walt is doing very well for what he has been through. Today he was able to get out of the hospital gown and put on regular clothes. He has taken two walks already and has had some physical therapy. He hasn't been back into his bed since he got dressed which is an improvement. To top it off, he even checked out his fantasy football on the computer.

This morning his surgeon Dr. Patel came in to see him and told him he could possibly go home tomorrow or Thursday. He was able to tell us a little more of Walt's issue. Apparently Walt had an aortic aneurysm, which caused the dissection. There is still a small tear in the upper aorta but the doctor felt he fixed everything that needed to be fixed right then. Walt will have yearly visits with this surgeon to monitor his heart. He reminded Walt that one in four patients with this condition never go home. We feel so blessed that God allowed us to have the surgery at U of M and we're so thankful for a surgeon at Genesys who let go of his pride, knew his limitations, and handed off the surgery. Now that this has all happened, we can look back over the past months and piece together events that happened to us and now realize that God was preparing us for this specific moment in our lives. I love the verse in James that says, "And the prayer offered in faith will make the sick person well, the Lord will raise him up ..."

During the afternoon on Tuesday, a volunteer from the hospital stopped by with a heart-shaped pillow. She asked me what had happened, and I explained my story to her. I will never forget her comment. She said, "The Lord must have something very special in store for you." Her comment made a large impression on me. This is the first time that I had heard anyone from the hospital make any mention of God, and it caught me by surprise.

On Tuesday evening, I got to see Gabe and Hope for the first time since the surgery. I missed my kids dearly, and I was anticipating the moment that I would get to see them. My mom, stepdad, Grandpa, Gabe, and Hope all came to visit. I will never forget the look that Hope gave me when she walked in. I don't think she was prepared to see her dad bundled in a chair with a big bandage on his neck and wires sticking out from everywhere. Hope was definitely a little afraid when she first saw me, but she warmed up quickly. I cannot place into words how good it was to be able to see and hug my kids. I know how fortunate I was to be alive. I wish it was easier to capture this moment and put it on paper, but it was very emotional. I do believe that we made the correct decision in not calling Gabe and Hope while I was about to go into surgery, as I would not have remembered it anyway, but I think it was a little difficult for the kids to grasp the severity of the situation since they were not closely attached to it from the beginning. I know that as they grow and hear the stories about God's miracle in my life, they will appreciate all that God did for our family.

Shortly after my kids arrived, three couples from our church came to visit. I remember being overwhelmed with having twelve people there all at once. But I do remember a moment when I looked around at everyone and felt blessed to have each and every one of them there with me. The visit took a lot out of me, but, once everyone had left, I was thankful for the friends and family that I have.

I was told that the plan was to discharge me on Wednesday, October 13, which was the following day. I remember thinking that I did not feel anywhere near ready to leave the hospital and the care that it provided. I didn't feel that I quite had a grasp on everything that had taken place to my body. I didn't believe that there was any way possible that I would be going home the next day. Besides, I was only four days removed from an eleven-hour open-heart surgery. I didn't think that they could possibly send me home so soon, and the anxiety started to set in.

Tuesday was an encouraging day with seeing Gabe and Hope and so many other visitors. Once everyone, including Sarah, had left for the night, I was overwhelmed with loneliness. I think it was a combination of all the commotion of the last few hours and then sudden quietness, as well as the trepidation of possibly going home the next day.

I could not sleep on Tuesday night. Reality was starting to sink in, and I was overwhelmed with the thoughts of what had happened to me. Prior to my surgery, my relationship with God was very important to me, and I felt as though that relationship was going tremendously. I was also committed to reading the Bible daily and felt as though I could talk to the Lord openly. As I was lying in my bed, I was trying to reach out to God. I assumed that I could easily talk to Him and ask Him why this had happened to me. I was frustrated by my inability to concentrate and to engage in a conversation with God. I felt very alone and cried off and on most of the night.

I was also struggling with the lack of knowledge of everything that had taken place with the dissection and surgery. I knew the basics, but I felt as though I did not have a firm grasp on everything in its entirety.

I was counting the minutes to when I could justify getting up and sitting in my chair. At approximately 7:30 a.m. on Wednesday, October 13, I got up and moved into the chair. I knew that Sarah would not be around for a couple of more hours, and I was having a very difficult time with the loneliness. At about 9:00 a.m., I closed my eyes and told the Lord that I was really lonely and did not want to be alone any longer. My eyes were closed for maybe fifteen minutes, and I got a sense that I was being watched. I slowly opened my eyes and saw, standing on the other side of the bed, my friend Matt from church. I was overwhelmed with God's answer to my prayer. Matt said that he thought I was sleeping. I explained to him the tough night that I just had and how lonely I was. I told him that I was not sleeping but was praying for the loneliness to go away.

This was a moment that really sticks out in my mind. I was struggling with reconnecting with God in the way that I had prior to my dissection, and He answered a very specific prayer almost immediately.

Chapter Thirteen

Discharged

THE IDEA OF GOING HOME ON this day continued to consume me. I was so happy that Matt had stopped by, and I explained to him that I did not want to go home today. It was encouraging to be able to be honest with someone about how I was feeling.

Thirty minutes after Matt stopped in, Dr. Patel came by to check on me. I was so happy that Matt was there, because I knew that Dr. Patel would be giving me some information and I was afraid that I might forget some of the details.

I explained how I had had a really rough night emotionally and did not want to go home today. Dr. Patel asked me probably the toughest question that could have been asked of me at that moment. He asked me why I did not want to go home. Honestly, I did not have a good answer for this. I told Dr. Patel that I just felt as though I needed another day in the hospital.

Dr. Patel very bluntly explained that with the sort of surgery that I underwent, there is always some form of depression that eventually presents itself. He wanted me to go home as soon as possible and get back around my family and any form of routine. This would be best for my mental state. Dr. Patel explained that I could either view this as a cup half full or a cup half empty. I could either focus heavily on what happened to me, or

I could appreciate that I did not die and leave my wife and children. If I continued to focus too much on all the negative aspects of what happened to me, I would drive both myself and my family crazy. The end result of the conversation was that as long as there were no complications, I was going to go home at some point on that day.

After he left, I looked at Matt without really knowing what to say. That was a lot of information to consume all at once.

Shortly after Dr. Patel left, Sarah arrived. I again was happy that Matt had been there when Dr. Patel was visiting with me, as it helped provide another set of ears. Matt visited for a little while longer and then left.

Sarah helped me clean up and get dressed for the day. We visited and sat around while waiting for the discharge news. I used this time to catch up on messages that were left on my cell phone and computer. I *again* was overwhelmed with the show of support that was coming our way. I will forever cherish the moments that I read through new messages, as they gave me such a huge lift during a time when I needed it the most.

When 3:30 p.m. rolled around, we received the news from our nurse that the discharge process had started. I was both excited and scared. I could not believe that just five days ago I was fighting for my life with an aorta dissection, and now I was going home. The next hour and a half was spent filling out paperwork and asking questions. There were a few medications that I would need to take, and those would have to be filled once I got home.

At 5:00 p.m., the nurse loaded me up in the wheelchair while Sarah went ahead to get the car. As I was sitting in my wheelchair in the lobby, with the nurse holding on, I was full of many emotions. Sarah finally pulled up to the door, and I remember the splash of fresh cold air on my face. It had seemed like forever since I had been outside.

It was so hard for me to get out of the wheelchair and into the car. There was so much weakness. I remember thinking how tough this was going to be. I finally got situated in the car, and we were on the road on our way home. The drive would take a little over an hour. It was raining heavily and there was a lot of traffic—everyone was heading home from work. Every bump seemed to hurt just a little more. I held the heart-shaped pillow between the seat belt and my chest. I tried to move as little as possible.

My entrance home was not as I would have expected. A few miles from home, we received a call from Amanda, Sarah's sister-in-law who had been staying at our house and watching the kids. Our home security alarm was going off and the alarm company was calling our house and my cell phone. Sarah gave Amanda the alarm code and instructions to tell the alarm company. It dawned on me that it was raining really hard, and our security alarm is hooked up to our sump pump in case the water level reached a certain point. Sarah asked Amanda to look at the sump pump, and, sure enough, it wasn't working.

As I entered the house, the aroma of freshly baked cookies filled the air. Sarah and Amanda immediately attempted to figure out what was going on with the sump pump as the alarm kept going off. There was a lot of chaos at the time, but it didn't seem to bother me. I felt helpless, as I was unable to do anything. I made my way to the couch to lie down. I was overwhelmed with emotions of actually being home and seeing my kids in their own environment, but I could not appreciate it as much as I would have liked due to my weakness and exhaustion.

Sarah called my brother, and both he and his father-in-law quickly arrived at our house to assess the sump pump situation. I am so thankful for their willingness to come over so quickly. The sump pump had stopped working, and they were able to purchase a new one. They hooked it up in no time.

The rest of the early evening consisted of Amanda feeding the kids and Sarah tracking down all my medications. Sarah had to go to multiple places to get all the medications, and I knew that it was stressful for her. As I was fading in and out on the couch, there seemed to be a lot going on around me, but it seemed to be nothing but a blur.

Once the kids were in bed and everything was quiet, Amanda, Sarah, and I sat and visited for awhile. I remember and appreciated this time of fellowship. I was happy to be home, but the weight of the recovery that was in front of me was overbearing.

Amanda offered to stay and help out for the next few days. As much as we would have liked her to stay, we felt as though she had made such a huge sacrifice already and knew that it would be best if she went back home to Cleveland. Amanda is one of the kindest people that I know, and I cannot appropriately convey how much we appreciated what she did for our family through the first several days of this most difficult time. Both Amanda and Sarah's sister Lydia, who watched Gabe and Hope in the beginning, were a tremendous encouragement to us.

My brother had moved my favorite recliner from the basement up to the family room so that I could sleep and sit in it. The first night was a rough one. I was in a lot of pain, and trying to sleep in the recliner was difficult. I felt insecure trying to lie down on the couch and obviously could not make it up the stairs to our bedroom. I was on some strong pain medications and needed them every four hours. I have had many muscle pulls and even a couple of muscle tears, but the pain that I was experiencing in my sternum was unlike anything I had felt before. Sarah slept on the couch that was close by. Needless to say, I did not get much sleep that first night.

I was only able to sleep in the recliner for the first couple of nights. The recliner was relaxing to rest on during the day, but I was having a very difficult time sleeping in it. The pain medications that I was on were very strong, and every four hours I was ready for my next dose. The second night sleeping in the recliner, I remember opening my eyes in the middle of the night and seeing our artificial tree in the corner of the family room start to move and come at me. I know that I had Sarah concerned at that point. I struggled for awhile with blurred vision and nightmares while on the pain medications. After this incident, I moved onto the couch, and Sarah moved over to the love seat. I had to stay in a prone position and this caused me a lot of difficulty sleeping. There was a time that I felt like it would be weeks before I had the courage to go up the stairs, but I was anxious to get into my own bed. Within a matter of days, I was able to do just that.

So many things that I took for granted were now difficult and frustrating. Getting out of my chair and going to the bathroom was a chore. For the first several days, I was not able to get into the shower, so I had to use a wash cloth to rinse myself down each morning. I was unsteady on my feet. Everything that I did took a lot of time. On many occasions, I would just burst out weeping. I would think about how I was riding my bike twenty miles a day, several days a week prior to the surgery, and now I could barely give myself a sponge bath. It took its toll on me emotionally.

There is a song that I have always loved, and during the last couple of days in the hospital I would repeat the lyrics in my head and weep repeatedly. The song talks about praising God even through the storm, and how God remains continually by your side.

The get-well cards came in the mail daily, along with visits and messages. All of this continued to be an encouragement to me. Not too long after I had been home from the hospital, I received a card in the mail from my stepbrother and sister-in-law who live out of state. When I opened the card, the song that meant so much to me in the hospital started to play. There are a few tear stains on that card. It was yet another example of how the Lord used someone to encourage me at exactly a time when I needed it the most.

One of Sarah's friends had coordinated a schedule for anyone who wanted to bring us meals, and we were very thankful for that. People brought meals over for nearly two weeks, and it was a tremendous help. The outpouring of support through phone calls, cards, flowers, and meals continued to pour in, and each time I felt blessed to have so many people showing us how much they loved and cared for us.

I was struggling both emotionally and mentally. Every night that I went to bed, I had thoughts that I might not wake up the next morning. I started realizing that I might never be able to ride my bike the way that I would like or play softball again. I was feeling guilty with worrying about these things when I should have just been appreciative that I was alive. As time went on, I felt as though I was never going to get better and would never feel normal again. I kept hearing people tell me that I just needed to give it time, and sometimes I just wanted to scream. These are the thoughts that I was struggling with daily, and they wore on me emotionally.

I would hear so many times how God must have something special planned for me, and I struggled with being clueless as to what that something special might be. I felt as though everyone knew something that I didn't, and I wondered what I was missing. I started to believe that if something special didn't happen, and soon, then I would let a lot of people down. Could there possibly be something spiritually wrong with me if something obviously big didn't happen? The pressure became too much to bear, and it was driving a wedge between God and me. I was already struggling with my relationship with Him, and this certainly did not help.

It was frustrating for me to be so debilitated. Although we had a lot of support, life still had to go on. Gabe and Hope had homework that they needed help with, lessons to be taken to, and school. Whenever there was a discipline issue, and Sarah was battling with it, I felt so useless. Not only was I unable to engage in any battles, but I also needed to be careful not to allow myself to get too worked up about anything. I needed to try to stay relaxed, and that was difficult at times. I felt bad that Sarah was on her own with Gabe and Hope, but, through much prayer, she did a fabulous job.

Several family and friends stopped by over the first few days that I was home. It was overwhelming at times, but I enjoyed and appreciated every moment of it. I felt that I needed to be around people as much as possible in order for me not to have too much down time to think about myself and the difficult road ahead. As the days wore on, the pain became more frustrating. Being in pain day in and day out, all day every day, was starting to wear on me.

On Monday, October 18, Sarah had to go back to work. I was not looking forward to her being gone during the day, but I had plenty of company. My grandpa came over nearly every day for awhile, and I thoroughly enjoyed my time with him. My grandpa had had open-heart surgery several years prior. I have to admit that open-heart surgery is not one of the things that I thought I would ever have in common with my grandfather.

I remember thinking about all the time that I was going to have while I was on my back in the recliner. I thought about how much book reading I could get done, and I was looking forward to being back in Scripture. I was both surprised and frustrated when the motivation was not there to do either. Prior to the surgery, I looked forward to starting my days in the Scriptures and was really frustrated with my inability to concentrate long enough to get back into the Word, considering all the time that I now had. I was also having a hard time talking to God about anything, let alone asking Him why this had happened to me. Even though I was having a difficult time entering into a conversation with God, I always felt that He was there with me and had not left me. I spoke to very few people about this, as I considered it a close, personal issue.

Sometimes when I was sitting all alone in the quietness, I would think about what it would be like for my wife and kids if I had died. Those thoughts put a lot of emotional strain on me, because I realized that I was so close to death. My thoughts quickly turned to how the Lord spared my life, which has allowed me more opportunity to spend time with my family.

I had targeted October 25 as the day that I would start working again. This was less than three weeks after my surgery, but I did not feel that my job would be stressful enough to keep me away from it much longer than this. I had asked the doctor about my work prior to leaving the hospital and was told that it would be okay as long as I listened to what my body was telling me. If I felt as though I was getting worked up, then it was very important that I take a break.

On November 11, I was scheduled to see my surgeon for the first time since my surgery. I was not allowed to drive before this appointment unless I received clearance. I also had an appointment with my new cardiologist on November 24.

As I mentioned earlier, I was having a hard time getting back into Scripture. I had difficulty concentrating on much of anything. I always took notes during my daily reading of the Bible. I had taken notes on October 7, the night that I went into the emergency room. I read Proverbs 10 and 11 on that day and took specific notes on several verses. I started taking notes again on October 18 when I read Proverbs 12. I took notes specifically on verses 1, 8, and 15. A lot had happened during that eleven-day gap, and I enjoy looking back at my notes on October 18 and seeing how God started to walk me through some of my difficulties simply by reading His Word.

Up to this point, I had not felt like being on the computer, but, on October 20, I took the time to write a brief story about my dissection for my Facebook page. I made it a point to thank everyone who was praying for me. I received numerous responses to that first post, and I get emotional each time that I read through them.

October 24 was the day that I wanted to go to church for the first time since my surgery. There was a special presentation on prayer that particular morning, and I wanted to be there and see it. It was very difficult to get up and get myself together, but it felt good to be out. I went into the service a little late and left a little early. I was very weak and did not think that I could handle talking too much. I was happy to be back in church where so many people had rallied around me and prayed for me and my family. I spent much time thinking about how two weeks prior I was fighting death, and now I was out and in church.

On Sunday evening, October 24, there was a business meeting at church. Even though I was exhausted from getting up and to church earlier that same morning, I wanted to be there for the meeting. I was on the ballot to serve as deacon. I had accepted the nomination over a month ago after spending time in prayer. At this point, I was ready to accept whatever happened. Even though I was in rough shape, I was still ready and willing to serve. After the ballots were cast, I had been voted in as a deacon. I was humbled that the Lord would allow me to serve my church in this position.

Chapter Fourteen

✝

Recovery

I STARTED TO FOCUS ON MY future quality of life. I was trying not to be too negative, but at the same time I needed to face reality. Reality was telling me that I could face difficulties because of this condition. I focused on certain dates that I wanted to make it to and appreciate. The first one was Halloween. I know the kids enjoy Halloween, and usually my brother, sister-in-law, and their two girls come over for pizza and trick or treating. This is something that we have done for a few years in a row, and I was yearning for something routine.

I made it to Halloween, and although I was not able to go trick or treating with the kids, I enjoyed having everyone around. My parents, grandpa, brother, sister-in-law, and two nieces all came over and we had a lot of fun.

I was warned about the severe depression that could develop after a tragedy such as the one that I had. A friend of mine recommended a Christian psychiatrist. Initially I didn't like the idea of seeing a psychiatrist, but I knew that I was struggling with a lot of things and realized that it would be a good idea to see if it could help. I had never been to a psychiatrist before, and I felt uncomfortable. It was a Thursday morning, just a few days before my first appointment in Ann Arbor to see my surgeon. The session went well, and some things were said that were a tremendous help to me. I did attend two more sessions and have not gone since then. I felt the psychiatrist was helpful to me, but I was not comfortable enough to continue making appointments.

On November 3, I developed a very uncomfortable flutter in my chest. It was fluttering every third or fifth beat and at times felt like my heart would jump out of my chest. Sarah made a phone call to the hospital in Ann Arbor. Someone at that hospital called my local family doctor to schedule an appointment for that same day to have an EKG done. The EKG results checked out fine, and I was scheduled to go to a local cardiology clinic and get fitted for a Holter Heart Monitor, which I would need to wear for twenty-four hours. On Monday, November 8, I went into the cardiology clinic and was quickly fitted with the heart monitor. Along with wearing the heart monitor, I had to chart each time that I felt the flutter. The fluttering was consistent, and the following morning I went back to the clinic to have the heart monitor removed.

On November 11, 2010, was my first appointment to see Dr. Patel since my surgery. When Dr. Patel walked into the room, he asked how I was doing. It was obvious that I was discouraged, and I did not try to hide that fact. Dr. Patel always has been honest without holding anything back, which I appreciated. With Sarah by my side, Dr. Patel again reiterated that when people have the type of dissections that I had, 90 percent of them don't make it. For those that do actually make it into the hospital, 25 percent of them don't make it out.

Dr. Patel reminded me that not only had I made it to the hospital, but I made it through the surgery and home with my family. I was now sitting there with him and Sarah talking about my recovery. I think this was one of those *You had to be there moments* to fully understand how humbling it truly was. Dr. Patel continued by saying that I now had a medical condition, would always have a medical condition, and the sooner I came to grips with this fact the better. It may sound harsh, but it is something that I needed to hear that day.

Even though I had a good conversation with Dr. Patel and was told that, as of now, everything was progressing well, I still felt as though I didn't have a firm grasp of the medical knowledge of everything that had happened to me; I felt unfulfilled. It was frustrating leaving the appointment having asked a lot of questions yet still feeling as though there was so much more that I needed to know.

As far as my sternum and other incisions, those were all healing on schedule. I asked again about the tear that was still on another part of my aorta. Dr. Patel explained that the tear was farther down on the trunk of the aorta. There is a small possibility that this tear can heal, although this is doubtful. If the tear gets worse, I will have to undergo an additional open-heart surgery. The knowledge of this additional tear is something that is constantly on my mind. It drives me crazy at times thinking about it.

I also informed Dr. Patel that I was still taking the pain medications that I had left the hospital with. These were very strong medications, and he informed me that I should no longer be taking these. He recommended that I start taking Extra Strength Tylenol in place of the narcotics immediately.

I was told that I would be facing lifetime restrictions. Dr. Patel did not detail any restrictions other than heavy lifting, but it was enough information to add to my mounting frustrations. He scheduled me for a follow-up appointment in February. I hoped to have a better idea of where I was in the healing process at that time. Just prior to seeing Dr. Patel, I had an EKG test. The results of that test did show the irregular heartbeats that I was experiencing. Dr. Patel explained that these were PVCs or premature ventricular contractions. These irregular heartbeats can occur in normal healthy people, but, since I just recently had major surgery near my heart, Dr. Patel referred me to an electrophysiologist at the University of

Michigan hospital. An appointment was made with the electrophysiologist for December 2.

On November 13, I decided to start a blog detailing my journey. There were so many people that were praying for me and wanted to know how I was progressing in my recovery, and I figured that a blog would be the best way to keep as many people notified as possible. I am happy to have so many people praying, and I am happy to let people know in which ways I need specific prayers.

It had now been five weeks since the surgery. I was trying to manage my pain with the Extra Strength Tylenol that my surgeon had recommended. The Tylenol did not even come close to dulling my pain. I needed to take the medicine every four hours, and rarely did it alleviate the pain. I struggled with quitting my pain medications. At the beginning, I had to sneak a few of the original pain medications along with my Tylenol. After a few weeks, the Tylenol started to work a bit better, as my sternum was healing.

The next couple of weeks were extremely frustrating. My premature ventricular contractions were acting up, my pain management was not going well, and I was experiencing intense fatigue. It was hard for me to be encouraged even if I had a good day. It seemed that many times when I took a step forward physically, the next couple of days would be steps backward.

My next focus date was Thanksgiving. I had an appointment with my new cardiologist in Ann Arbor the day before Thanksgiving and was hoping that this would provide additional information about my surgery and recovery process.

On November 15, I started picking the kids up from school. Before the surgery, the normal routine was for me to take them to school in the morning and pick them up. After the surgery, Sarah had been taking them to school in the morning, a little earlier than normal, and then they would stay in latchkey until Sarah picked them up after she got out of work. I was in desperate need of some sense of routine, and picking the kids up from school provided me with a sense of accomplishment. I felt as though this was a big step forward in my recovery. It sounds silly that picking Gabe and Hope up from school would be a step forward in my recovery process, but I was struggling mentally.

I remember November 15 very well. I was anticipating getting into the car, driving to the school, and getting Gabe and Hope myself. At 3:00 p.m., I saw Hope come out of school. I got out of the car so that she could see me. As soon as Hope saw me, she started to run at me, which is what she did every day before my surgery. As soon as she was almost in my arms, I had to turn away so that she would not leap into my arms. The moment I turned, it dawned on me that I would never be able to lift my children up and hold them again. This was a very difficult moment for me, and it is something that I still struggle with today. Both Gabe and Hope are young enough that, if I wasn't recovering from open-heart surgery, I could still pick them up and horse around with them.

Another thing that I struggled with on November 15 was that this was the day I would normally be up north with my grandpa and brother for opening day of deer hunting season. Many of the fond memories that I have of growing up and becoming a man were the weekends spent at the hunting cabin. As I got older, I didn't have to be a successful hunter to enjoy and appreciate the time I was up at the cabin. Being with my grandpa and brother and enjoying God's creation and the quietness of the outdoors was what I considered success. It was difficult not being up north and realizing that I would be missing an entire season at the hunting cabin. I can only hope and pray that I will be well enough to make the trip next year.

The fatigue that I had been experiencing was getting worse, yet at the same time I was having trouble getting any sleep. Each day was increasingly frustrating. I was looking forward to meeting with my cardiologist on the twenty-fourth of November.

The electrophysiologist requested that I have an echocardiogram done prior to my appointment with him in December. The echocardiogram was scheduled at a local cardiologist clinic on November 19. Several days leading up to the nineteenth, my blood pressure was running consistently high. Blood pressure is an area that is going to be very important to keep under control for the rest of my life. My blood pressure needs to be below 130 in order to keep the strain off my aorta. For the last several days, it was running consistently above 130.

I was not having a good day on the day of my echocardiogram appointment. My blood pressure was still consistently high, and I was struggling mightily with my fatigue issues. Just before leaving for my appointment, I did a quick check of my blood pressure. The reading was 169, which is way too high for where I need to be.

I left for my echocardiogram. When I went into the room to have the test done, I informed them that my blood pressure was reading high. They checked it themselves, and it was still reading in the 160s. The person conducting the test said that they would finish the test and then check my blood pressure again.

I did not enjoy the echocardiogram. I had to remove my shirt, and I was already self-conscious about my large ugly scar as it was. I had to lie in different positions, which was uncomfortable because of my sternum discomfort, and a computer-looking mouse contraption was rubbed around on my chest and ribs.

Once the test was over, the technician rechecked my blood pressure. It was still exactly 169. The clinic was not comfortable sending me home with a blood pressure reading that high, so staff called my family doctor to see if they could send me right over. My doctor's office was closed for lunch. The clinic's staff asked me to go immediately to my doctor's office, and they would continue calling.

By the time I arrived at the doctor's office, my doctor and his staff were back for lunch, but they had not spoken to anyone at the clinic as of yet. I explained the situation to them. I only needed to wait for about twenty minutes and then was called back to meet with my doctor. My blood pressure was again checked, and it was still reading higher than what it should be. My doctor decided to double my dose of blood pressure medication in order to get my blood pressure down as quickly as possible.

Once I left my doctor's office, I called Ann Arbor and asked if doubling my blood pressure medication was the appropriate thing to do. I was informed that I needed to wait for at least one full day and to continue checking my blood pressure to see if it would go down on its own. By that same evening, my pressure had begun to lower to an acceptable level. I did not need to double my medication. The whole process put a strain on me mentally, and I was relieved to see my blood pressure come done on its own.

The past several days had been rough. There were three main areas that affected me: pain, blood pressure, and the premature ventricular contractions. I had problems with at least one of them daily, and it was wearing me down emotionally.

The Lord knew that I was suffering mentally, and, between November 19 and my cardiologist appointment on November 24, I was receiving a lot of phone calls, text messages, and emails, all at just the right moments. Since I was now able to drive, and felt more comfortable getting around, I began to meet some friends for lunch. That provided much needed encouragement.

My cardiologist appointment on November 24 was finally here. Sarah took part of the day off work, and we drove down to Ann Arbor to meet with my new cardiologist. This particular cardiologist specializes in aortic diseases, and I am thankful that the Lord opened the doors to allow me to connect with her. Sarah and I are so thankful that we were recommended to the doctors at the U of M hospital, and feel that my care is in the best of hands.

During my appointment, I asked a lot of questions and walked away with a much clearer understanding about what had happened to me and where I should go from here. I suffered a type A aortic dissection, which involves the ascending aorta and the aortic arch. Part of my descending aorta also tore and remains torn. The damaged portion of my ascending aorta was removed and replaced with a graft, while the portion of my descending aorta that is still torn will be closely monitored for the rest of my life.

I also asked the cardiologist about my fatigue that was continuing to get worse. The cardiologist informed me that this is normal specifically with the type of surgery that I had. At least I had some answers as to why I was so tired all of the time, but I would have to deal with it for several months.

I was really missing riding my bike and took this opportunity to talk to my cardiologist about it. I told her that I could set my bike up on an indoor trainer and was wondering if I could start riding it. The cardiologist said that as long as I take it easy, and ride no more than thirty minutes a day, then I could start riding my bike again. I was excited.

Sarah and I went to lunch after the appointment and had a good conversation about all the information that we just took in. I did feel that I was beginning to get a clearer picture of what happened and what to expect, but it did not erase some of my fears, not the least of which was the tear that was still on my aorta.

The following day was Thanksgiving, which was my next focus point. My aunt and uncle from Florida were in town, and we had everyone over for Thanksgiving dinner at our house. It was great to be with family on Thanksgiving, and I certainly had a lot to be thankful for. Thanksgiving was a relaxing day filled with great food and a lot of football. I was still very tired all of the time, but being with family helped take my mind off some of my worries for a short period of time.

A few days after my appointment with my cardiologist, I received a call from their office with the results of the echocardiogram that I had done locally on November 19. The results of the test showed mild aortic insufficiency, which was positive news.

As soon as I could, I set my bike up on the indoor trainer in the basement. The anticipation was high for the first ride, but the mood changed from excitement to overwhelming frustration by the time the first ride was over. Prior to my surgery, I was riding twenty minutes a few days per week, and on this first ride, it took me fifteen minutes to go two miles. (I almost had to read that last sentence again just to believe it.) I realize what my body has been through, and I need to give myself some time, but it was very frustrating nonetheless. My goal was to keep riding each day for at least fifteen minutes.

My next focus point was my birthday, which was on December 3, but first we had an appointment on December 2 with the electrophysiologist. My premature ventricular contractions were getting worse, and I was hoping to get some clear answers about what we can do about them.

The first thing the doctor said when she walked into the room was, "I know a lot about you even though I haven't met you." She mentioned that my surgeon, Dr. Patel, had asked her to see me as soon as possible.

The doctor explained everything very well, and I came loaded with a lot of questions. She explained that with the severity of the surgery that I had, it is not uncommon to develop premature ventricular contractions. The trauma from both the dissection and the surgery can cause one's heart to be knocked off course. It is possible for the premature ventricular contractions to slowly get better and possibly stop altogether as everything continues to heal. What doctors want to see is for the premature ventricular contractions to be less than 10 percent of a person's heartbeats. Once the premature ventricular contractions get to 10 percent or greater, then measures would need to be taken to correct the problem. The worst case scenario would be a heart ablation. The first EKG that they saw from me a few weeks ago showed an extra heartbeat every other beat, roughly 50 percent of my heartbeats. The EKG that they took the day of my appointment rarely showed an extra heartbeat. The electrophysiologist scheduled me for an appointment in February to be fitted with another Holter Heart Monitor, which I would wear for a full forty-eight hours. The results would be evaluated to see if the premature ventricular contractions were getting any better. I was told that the premature ventricular contractions, under my circumstances, could last three to six months. I would continue to be monitored during this period. A course of action, if any, would be decided based upon the results of the testing that would take place over the course of the next few months.

I was given a very accurate explanation from the electrophysiologist of the seriousness of my aorta aneurysm, which caused my aorta dissection. The doctor said it was a very large aneurysm and that I was extremely fortunate. When my aorta dissected, it was bad enough to fill many of the layers of my aorta, and it bulged just to the point of bursting. Each time I was told by a doctor how fortunate I was, and the seriousness of my dissection, it made me want to continue to thank God for saving my life.

My birthday was on December 3, and Sarah and I went to a restaurant recommended by a friend. The place where we went was a forty-five-minute drive, but the food was well worth it. I was having a bad day with my fatigue. With the drive to the restaurant, eating, and the drive back, I tried hard to stay alert and awake. The fatigue that I continued to experience was extremely frustrating.

On December 7, I had an appointment in Ann Arbor with the Cardiovascular Medicine Group to better educate me about my blood pressure control. Just like the previous doctors, this doctor reiterated how lucky I was that I survived my dissection. He was surprised that I had a dissection at my young age and without showing signs of any of the normal factors that cause many of the dissections. These factors included genetics, chronic high blood pressure, or a common disease. We spent a lot of time going over my blood pressure requirements, and what my blood pressure means to my heart and aorta. I was overwhelmed with all the information but was very pleased with the thoroughness.

The doctor also made some prescription changes. He doubled the dose of my blood pressure medication, which allowed me to take it only once a day instead of twice a day as before. He also changed the beta blocker medication I was on to a newer medicine, which also allowed me to take it once a day. He explained that this beta blocker lowers blood pressure in two different ways. It lowers my normal outer pressure like the one you take from your arm, yet it keeps the pressure around my aorta a different, lower pressure. Another way he explained it is that the medication keeps my heart from banging too hard on my aorta. This sort of technology amazes me. I thank God daily for leading me to Ann Arbor and this whole group of doctors. They are all certainly cutting edge.

Once I was finished with the Cardiovascular Medicine Group appointment, I knew I was in the clear from any further appointments in Ann Arbor until February 3, 2011, when I would have my first CAT scan since my surgery. This would give a clear picture of how my aorta was healing. Along with my CAT scan, I also had an echocardiogram scheduled. Then on February 10, I would go back to see my surgeon and cardiologist to discuss the test results.

My current plan was to continue to recover and ride my bike as much as my body would allow. I was still having a hard time with my fatigue, but riding my bike consistently seemed to be helping. I was also beginning to sleep better, and my eyes were now set on getting to Christmas with some positive recovery.

Chapter Fifteen

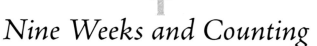

Nine Weeks and Counting

IT HAD NOW BEEN NINE WEEKS since the surgery. The pain was starting to show improvement, but it was still always there. Being in pain daily for nine consistent weeks was putting a lot of pressure on me emotionally. At this point, I was taking it one day at a time and looking forward to Christmas.

I had never heard of an aorta dissection prior to it happening to me, and then, on December 11, I read on the Internet that a well-known political person had been admitted to the hospital with an aorta dissection. I have to admit that seeing this brought a lot of emotions. I followed the story closely each day. On December 13, I saw a report that he had passed away from complications due to his dissection. Even though I did not know this person, and he was older than I am—he was sixty-nine—it still overwhelmed me with emotions.

Each day I had some small episode that concerned me. My blood pressure would be too high or too low, I would get some strange chest pains, or my premature ventricular contractions would start acting up. We had to make a few phone calls to Ann Arbor on occasions, but I tried really hard not to run to the emergency room with each ache or pain. Sometimes it was very hard not to go to the hospital. I kept reminding myself of Psalm 121:2: "My help comes from the Lord, the Maker of heaven and earth."

Just prior to my dissection, the Room of Grace, which was being held at my brother's church and had started in February, was on hold. A couple of guys were going to be gone for an extended period of time, and I thought it would be good to take a few weeks off. Back in October 2009, I started talking to some of the leaders at my church about having a Room of Grace there. I shared my passion with as many people as I could, and a few meetings about the Room of Grace had been held. I had experienced firsthand how important it was for men to get together, without a firm agenda, and share with each other what our struggles were. Men need an environment where they can leave their masks behind and show other men their true identity, and in turn they will be there for one another.

Proverbs 28:13 says, "Whoever conceals their sins does not prosper, but the one who confesses and renounces them finds mercy."

I felt that a good place to start a Room of Grace was at my church, and I felt called by the Holy Spirit to move in that direction.

On December 14, I was called in to meet with the elder board to answer some questions about the Room of Grace. I felt as though I appropriately shared my passion for men, and, later on that evening, I received a call from my friend Matt who serves on the elder board. He let me know that the Room of Grace had been approved. We prepared to start in the middle of February, and I was really excited to see how God would use this ministry.

As Christmas got closer, my emotions were all over the place. Usually as Christmas gets nearer, I tend to get very excited myself, but this year it was different. I had an *I can take it or leave it* attitude. I know that the true reason for Christmas is to celebrate Christ's birth, but I was just not excited. And I did not like the way I was feeling. I was still excited for Gabe and Hope and felt the joy that they were displaying. I was refusing to be the guy who walked around and looked sad all the time. I was trying my best to put on a happy face and was hoping that I could regain in time for the holidays some of the joy that I had lost.

On December 18, I went on my annual shopping trip with my mom. Each year, we have a tradition of going out to dinner together, and I would Christmas shop for Sarah while my mom would finish any additional shopping that she may have left. This year we decided to start the day off on a Saturday afternoon so that we had more time, and I would not have to be out too late. I was still suffering from a lot of fatigue, and I was not sure how good I would do on this shopping trip. We ate lunch and then began shopping. My body did really well, and I was pleasantly surprised. By the time the day had ended, we had shopped for nine hours and had eaten dinner as well. I woke up on Sunday and felt great. However, on Monday, December 20, the long day of shopping a couple of days ago caught up to me. I woke up tired, sore, and just not feeling very well. And my premature ventricular contractions were acting up worse than normal. This was a rude reminder of the limitations of my body.

Just before Christmas, I reached out to a couple of people and got the names of the doctors who were on duty when I went into the emergency room on October 8 so I could write personal letters thanking them for everything that they had done for me. I have no doubts that God placed the right people there for me on that night. One of the biggest reasons that people often die when suffering from an aorta dissection is that it's difficult to diagnose. There were three doctors on duty that day, which made a large impact on me.

The doctor that broke the news of my diagnosis was a very kind individual who had already made an impact on me prior to telling me the news of my dissection. I also wanted to write a letter to the doctor who ordered the CAT scan, as that could have very well been the test that saved my life. The third doctor was the surgeon on duty that evening. He could have easily attempted the surgery, but he set aside his pride and made the call to send me to the University of Michigan hospital as this was in my best interest. I also sent a letter to my surgeon, Dr. Patel, and thanked him for having a part in saving my life. I truly appreciated each and every one of these doctors and I wanted to show them that appreciation.

Christmas turned out to be a good day. I appreciated just lying around the house and being with my family. I could not help but soak in the fact that there was a really good chance of me not being here for this special day, and so I enjoyed seeing my children so happy. The small things that I tended to take for granted I now appreciate more and more each and every day. I appreciate eating dinner each night with our family around the table. I enjoyed playing chess and foosball with Gabe during his Christmas break. I also felt well enough to play Wii with Gabe, usually getting beaten badly. There were times that I would find Hope and just sit with her for a while and talk. I have a fresh appreciation for my family and what they mean to me.

While in the hospital toward the end of my stay, I remember one evening, late at night, while all alone and realizing the severity of everything that had happened to me and my future quality of life. I grasped the reality that there is a good chance that I will not be around for very long, so I need to appreciate each and every day. One of those days was Christmas.

On December 27, I started reading the book of Ecclesiastes, which is a sermon by Solomon, and read these verses from 2:10–11:

> I denied nothing my eyes desired;
> I refused my heart no pleasure.
> My heart took delight in all my work,
> and this was the reward for all my labor.
> Yet when I surveyed all that my hands had done
> and what I had toiled to achieve,
> everything was meaningless, a chasing after the wind;
> nothing was gained under the sun.

Christmas of 2010 was now over, and I was anticipating ringing in 2011. Gabe and Hope were off school the week of the twenty-seventh and had been staying up late. Sarah and I were discussing whether or not we wanted to do anything for New Year's Eve but decided to stay home as a family since everyone was so tired. I was looking forward to ringing in the New Year peacefully and quietly with just my family. The year 2010 was one I would like to put behind me, and it was time to move forward.

Chapter Sixteen

Back to the Hospital

On Tuesday, December 28, I started feeling a pain in my upper right inner thigh. The pain was in a very small area and it was a stabbing pain. I was not sure what to think of the pain but assumed that it was muscle related. I had not been able to ride my bike for the last several days, so I was certain that I did not injure myself on the bike. By Wednesday, the pain had become almost unbearable. I did not feel any pain whatsoever while sitting or lying down. However, when I was walking, the pain would randomly hit me. By now it felt like a tearing pain. I continued to think that it must be muscle related and was hoping that it would go away.

On Thursday, December 30, I developed uncomfortable pains in my chest—they were not the normal sternum pain. As Thursday evening rolled around, we decided to go out to eat as a family. My leg was really bothering me, but I really wanted to go out to eat. We had picked a place that was about a half-hour drive away and headed out. About five minutes into the trip, my chest really started to bother me. I told Sarah that I was going to have to strongly consider a trip to the emergency room. I was starting to think about the fact that both my leg and chest had hurt within days of one another. I had been well educated about my aorta and knew that the aorta extends down to the stomach area and farther. I became concerned the more I thought about it and wondered if I was having a problem with either my heart or the aorta.

We decided to eat out anyway but went to a restaurant closer to home. By the time we had finished up our dinner, I told Sarah that I needed to drive to the emergency room. I called my mom and confirmed that we could drop off Gabe and Hope. It was now 7:00 p.m. and I had no idea what type of evening I had in store.

Sarah dropped me off at the entrance to the emergency room. My leg was really bothering me, so I did not want to have to park and walk a long distance. I proceeded to the front desk and checked in. Because of my history, I was in a room within ten minutes. Almost immediately after going into the back, an IV was placed in my arm. All the horrible memories of October 8 were rushing through my head at this point. I remember feeling bad for Sarah and the thought that this could turn into another long night. A few doctors and nurses that had been on duty during my dissection a few weeks earlier remembered me. I don't think that it is every day that they get someone who has an aorta dissection and have to airlift him away.

After all the initial stabilizing procedures and questions, I was taken for a CAT scan. Within ten minutes, after arriving back to my room from the CAT scan, I was taken to have a Doppler scan done on my leg in order to rule out a possible blood clot. The Doppler scan only took about fifteen minutes, and I was then taken back to my room where Sarah was waiting for me.

We waited for quite awhile to hear the results of the CAT scan and Doppler scan. The anticipation was overbearing. I was concerned about what might be going on and was thinking the worst. The worst possible scenario for me would be another open-heart surgery. Once in awhile, Sarah and I could hear the doctors talking outside the room and could hear my name, and the word *aorta*. Neither one of us wanted to catch bits and pieces of this sort of conversation, so I asked Sarah to shut the door.

After maybe an hour, the doctors entered the room. They explained that the Doppler scan was clear and there were no signs of a blood clot. But they were having a difficult time reading the CAT scan. The doctors explained that it could be because I was either dissecting again or it was just difficult for them to read because of the graft that had been done on the aorta. The doctors did not have any previous CAT scan to compare it to. They also contacted the cardiac surgeon who was currently on duty, and he too said that it would be difficult to read because the surgery had not been done at that particular hospital.

The next step was to contact my surgeon at the University of Michigan hospital and see what he wanted to do. After a little bit of a wait, the surgeon on call at the University of Michigan suggested that I be transported to their hospital so that they could look me over themselves.

When I heard this, my heart sank. It was two days before the New Year, and I was being taken back to Ann Arbor. I, and my little faith, assumed the worst, and I knew that I was in for a very long night. Now we needed to wait for the ambulance to arrive.

I was concerned about Sarah driving by herself, so we called my brother. He was going to come to the hospital and ride with Sarah to Ann Arbor. At approximately 12:30 a.m., on Friday, December 31, 2010, I was loaded up on an ambulance and on my way to Ann Arbor. I had a good conversation with the paramedic who rode in the back with me, and the trip seemed to go by faster than I expected.

At 1:15 a.m., I arrived at the emergency room at the University of Michigan hospital. When I was wheeled back into the curtain area, there was a large team waiting for me. It seemed like something out of a television show. By the looks of things, you would think that I was hanging on for dear life. Everyone jumped into action, and everything seemed to be happening very quickly. My anxiety level had risen considerably. The emergency room doctor asked a lot of questions, and blood was drawn for testing. A couple of the nurses on duty remembered me from my dissection. As I explained earlier in this story, I did not remember any of the trip to the emergency room on October 8, but, oddly enough, I recognized a couple of the voices. Once the initial tests and questions were done, Sarah and my brother were able to come back. It was such a relief to have the two of them with me.

The CAT scan from the hospital that I had just come from was waiting to be reviewed by the appropriate doctors. We waited for quite awhile, and, at about 4:00 a.m., the emergency room doctor stopped by to let me know that all the blood tests were fine, but we were still waiting for the CAT scan to be reviewed. The anticipation on whether or not something was seriously wrong with me was horrifying.

At approximately 4:30 a.m., one of the surgeons from the cardiac group stopped by. This was the surgeon who had talked to Genesys, and recommended that I be sent to Ann Arbor. The doctor explained that there was a suspicious spot in my groin area. Because of the chest pains, and the pain in my leg, there was a possibility that I could be dissecting in my groin area, but it could also just be a bad image from the CAT scan as well. Because of my history, they needed to make sure. There was a well-known doctor who was one of the best at reading these scans, and we were waiting for him.

At around 5:30 a.m., the surgeon came back and said that the picture had been reviewed: the suspicious spot was enough to keep me around. They wanted to give me a CAT scan of their own so that they could review it appropriately. When having a CAT scan, a dye substance is shot throughout your body, and it is not good for the kidneys. Since I had just had a CAT scan a few hours ago, they needed to wait a little more than a day before giving me another one. I was going to be admitted into the cardiothoracic ICU so that I could be closely monitored until another CAT scan could be given. While in the ICU, liquids were going to be given to me through my IV, as well as some additional medications to protect my kidneys. I was very disappointed because it was New Year's

Back to the Hospital

Eve and the ICU was not the place I wanted to be while ringing in the New Year.

By 6:00 a.m. I was in my room at the ICU. Sarah and my brother were still with me and I could tell that they were exhausted, as was I. Once I was settled into my room, they went home. Sarah said she was going to get a little bit of rest and would be back. Once everyone cleared out, I lay there, flat on my back, in disbelief that this nightmare was happening again. I knew that it was going to be hard to sleep, but I shut my eyes and tried.

I was awakened at 10:45 a.m. by one of the head doctors from the cardiac group. He asked me some questions and then explained in more detail what they found on the CAT scan. There were actually two suspicious spots. One was on the abdomen in addition to the one in the groin area. The doctor said that he felt that it was an imaging issue, but he could not be sure and he was not going to take any chances because of my history. The goal was to protect my kidneys and keep me stabilized until the next CAT scan could be conducted. The CAT scan was scheduled for the following day, January 1, 2011, but the doctors were not sure of the time as of yet. After the doctor left, I got out of bed, moved into the chair, and thought about all that was going on.

Friday was a very lonely day for me. I knew Sarah was not going to be back until later in the afternoon, as she needed to rest, and I was not anticipating any visitors. I spent the day just sitting quietly in my chair. The nurses were very nice. A couple of times, my nurse stopped in and said that she felt bad for me—each time she walked by my room, she would just see me staring into nowhere.

During the day, I was hydrated with fluids through an IV. I was also given a medicine that had the foulest-smelling odor I have ever smelled. It left an aftertaste that would not go away. This medicine was given to protect my kidneys. In addition to the kidney medications, I had to be given a Heparin shot every eight hours in my stomach in order to protect against blood clots. I have had many shots in my lifetime, but these stung unlike any shot I had ever been given before. Overall, it was just a bad day.

Sarah arrived at 3:00 p.m., and I was really glad to see her. I needed her presence and support more than ever. Sarah and I spent the day sitting around and waiting for news about when I would be getting my CAT scan. Sarah had reserved the hotel that was located on the University of Michigan campus, so I was happy that she could stay late and not have to drive all the way home. Even though this was not the ideal situation for ringing in the New Year, I was glad to be with Sarah when midnight rolled around. I was also missing Gabe and Hope. Soon after midnight came, Sarah left for her hotel room and I went to bed. I was extremely tired, and I was hoping to be able to get some much needed rest.

The nurse came in every two hours to check my vitals, so I was unable to get any consistent sleep, but I did sleep soundly between the nurse's visits. Unfortunately I had to get one of the Heparin shots at 6:00 a.m., so that was a rude awakening. I was up and ready to get out of bed by 7:00 a.m. Even though I did not get a whole lot of sleep, I did feel a little more rested. Sarah arrived shortly after I got up, and I was told that the CAT scan was scheduled for 9:00 a.m. I was glad to at least have a time that I could focus on. My brother and grandpa arrived a short time later.

On Saturday, January 1, 2011, at 9:00 a.m., the nurse moved me into a wheelchair and led me to the CAT scan room. This particular scan was going to cover a larger area in my chest, abdomen, and groin. Shortly after returning from the CAT scan, the doctor from the morning before stopped by and told me that it would be later that afternoon before the results were in. There were a couple of doctors that needed to read the scan, and it would take time before all of that could be accomplished. The anticipation was overwhelming.

At approximately 1:30 p.m., the nurse practitioner stopped by and excitedly told me the good news. Everything checked out fine, and there were no areas to be concerned about. My aorta was stable, and my discharge papers were going to be drawn up shortly. When the good news was given to me, Sarah, my brother, and grandpa were all gone to lunch. I texted Sarah that the results had come back and asked when she would be back. Sarah immediately called me and said that it was a long walk back from where they were eating and she wanted to know the news. We all were very relieved, and I thanked the Lord for His protection.

Nearly the same time that I was given the results, a friend called and said that he, his wife, and another couple from my church were coming to visit me. I shared the good news with him, and told him that I was going to be discharged soon. They decided to come and visit anyway since they were already on their way. It was exciting to be able to share with them the joy of leaving the hospital. We visited in the waiting room for a little while and then left for home.

The last trip to the hospital had a profound effect on me. Being back in the ICU, not being able to see my children, the lack of sleep, the pricks of needles, and just the overall experience of being there was really tough on me the second time around. I was extremely thankful that the tests came back negative, and I know that it was due to the power of prayer. The text and emails from people telling me they were praying for me were encouraging.

The pain in my leg was still there but did not seem as severe. I kept it tightly wrapped with a bandage, which allowed me to walk. The pain was not as consistent as it had been earlier, but when it hit, it was excruciating. I decided if it did not improve soon, I would make a trip to the doctor.

A call came from the University of Michigan hospital on January 6, 2011, letting me know that Dr. Patel confirmed that the CAT scan looked good and I would not need the CAT scan that was scheduled for February; they would still do the echocardiogram and have me fitted for a Holter Heart Monitor. I would then follow up with my cardiologist and surgeon on February 10, 2011. If everything looked good, and no additional complications arose, I would not have to go back to Ann Arbor for a year.

February 3 finally came. I had been anticipating this day and was anxious to get it out of the way so that I could get to February 10, which would be the day of visiting with my cardiologist and surgeon concerning my test results. Since we had a huge snowstorm on Tuesday night, February 1, Sarah was off work for a couple days and the kids were off from school. It was nice having my whole family home for a couple of days. I have a new perspective on family as well as on life ever since God allowed me to survive my aortic dissection.

Having everyone at home allowed us to travel to the University of Michigan hospital in Ann Arbor together. The original plan had me going by myself, and I was not looking forward to it.

Every time I go to the University of Michigan hospital, heaps of memories come crashing in on me. The time that I was at U of M for the dissection, I was flown in by helicopter, so I never saw the route that was taken to the hospital and I never saw much of the outside as well. The things that stick out in my memory were the smells, the paint on the walls, the uniforms of the doctors and nurses, and the sounds around me. Each time I go to the U of M hospital for appointments, all of these things are so vivid to me and have a rather large impact on me. This day was no exception. Whenever I am there, it is never an easy in and out. It is a painful reminder of everything that has taken place.

We arrived early for my echocardiogram. When I was called back, I asked Gabe if he would like to come with me and watch the test. I thought it would be interesting for him, as many kids his age are not able to see medical procedures such as this. Gabe seemed to give it some thought, but if I had to guess, he was probably a little nervous about it. After a few minutes of thinking, he said that he would rather not. Sarah took the kids to the cafeteria for some snacks while I went back for my test.

I had had an echocardiogram a few weeks earlier, and it was not a pleasant experience. I was further into my recovery since the last echo, and this time it was not as uncomfortable. I was still not thrilled about taking off my shirt while a computer-type contraption rubbed cold gel all around my sore sternum. The test lasted for thirty minutes. Once I was finished, I checked in at the front desk for my heart-monitor fitting.

Shortly after my echocardiogram, I was called back for my heart-monitor fitting. I was not excited to hear that the nurse was going to have to do a little bit of shaving in order for the probes to stick correctly. The nurse shaved a couple of spots on my chest, one of which was too close to my open heart surgery scar for my comfort. Four probes were placed on my chest and the heart monitor was officially turned on at 2:15 p.m. I was informed that I would have to wear the heart monitor until 2:15 p.m. on Saturday, February 5. I was also given a chart to record each time that I felt the premature ventricular contractions acting up along with the activity that I was engaged in at the time. I also had to record each time that I woke up in the morning and each time that I went to bed in the evening. After my forty-eight hours had passed, I was given a pre-stamped pouch that I had to place the heart monitor in, and then I had to mail it back to the hospital.

We decided to go out to a nice dinner on the way back home. As I sat with my family in the restaurant, I realized that underneath my shirt were several wires registering each of my heartbeats. I reflected on how thankful I was that God allowed me this extra time to spend with my family. Each day is tough in its own unique way, and I know that I have a long road ahead of me, but I am thankful for such a wonderful family that is on this journey along with me.

I remember all too well having to wear the Holter Heart Monitor for twenty-four hours several weeks ago, so I was not looking forward to adding an extra day to it. However, I realized that wearing the heart monitor is required for finding out how often my premature ventricular contractions are acting up. It was difficult to sleep on February 3 and 4. My mind was focusing too much on the heart monitor and I was hoping that the two days would go by quickly. On Friday night, February 4, Sarah and I went out for dinner, so that helped to take my mind off things for a little while. As soon as 2:15 p.m. came on Saturday, I could not get the heart monitor off quickly enough. I would be having an appointment in the upcoming weeks to find out the results.

February 10 was my next follow-up appointment in Ann Arbor to meet with both my cardiologist and my surgeon. The purpose of these appointments was to go over the echocardiogram as well as the CAT scan that was done on New Year's Day. The day of my appointment, I went loaded with many questions. My goal was to find out what restrictions I would continue to be under and to receive a better understanding of what I could look forward to in the upcoming months.

I was pleased with the results of my appointment. My cardiologist was able to show me a picture of my CAT scan and said everything looked stable. The tear that was not replaced during the surgery was still there but had not gotten any worse. My aortic valve was also leaking a little bit. Neither of these was currently life threatening. My cardiologist said that these issues would be monitored closely.

My originally scheduled electrophysiologist appointment for February was rescheduled for March 3. The purpose of this appointment was to find out the results of my Holter Heart Monitor test that I had a few weeks prior and to determine what course of action to take based from those results.

The results of my test showed that during the forty-eight hour period that I wore the heart monitor, I had approximately eleven thousand premature ventricular contractions. I was told that this amount was close to the 10 percent mark of my overall heartbeats.

The doctor informed me that I could try medication, have a cardiac ablation, or do nothing for the time being, and see if the PVCs continued to improve. I had not been bothered as much as in the past by the premature ventricular contractions and elected to try to tolerate them. I was informed that my progress would continue to be monitored by the electrophysiologist, and I was scheduled for a follow-up appointment in one year.

I was relieved that this appointment was now behind me, and no procedures were necessary. Going forward, I will continue seeing my doctors a couple times a year for checkups and will continue to trust God to take care of me.

Chapter Seventeen

What Now?

BEFORE MY SURGERY, I ENJOYED TALKING to God daily and seeing my relationship with Him continuing to grow. Once my dissection happened, I had a really hard time reconnecting with God. On October 18, 2010, I finally was able to concentrate enough to get back into the Word, but I was still having a hard time talking to God. I always felt as though He was right there with me, but I was frustrated with my inability to connect with Him. I was starting to pray more, but it was shallow. I could not connect on the inmate level that I was accustomed to prior to my surgery.

I was trying really hard to reconnect with God. Maybe I was trying too hard. I was expecting a *Wow!* moment.

As the weeks went by, this moment never happened, and my frustrations grew bigger. Each and every day was a struggle. I had a hard time understanding why it was so hard to talk to God as I had done often before my surgery. There were times that I wondered if maybe He was leaving me alone to figure this all out on my own, although I never did feel 100 percent left alone. It was as if He was right there by my side, telling me that whenever I was ready, we could talk. I was frustrated because I thought I was ready all along. God was waiting for His perfect timing.

I felt as though this was a very personal matter, and I talked to very few people about it.

In January, 2011, the moment that I was anticipating happened. I was not expecting it, and God started to speak to me. I felt as though He was bringing me close to His side and letting me know that not only did He never leave me, but He is with me now, hand in hand, and will guide me through the difficult times that are ahead of me. While sitting all alone in the quietness, God reached out His hand to me. I think this is exactly how He wanted the moment to be. I had never felt closer to the Lord than I did at that moment. It was a very emotional time for me, and I was weeping uncontrollably. It had taken over three months for my heart to be prepared and ready to have that conversation with God.

Maybe the reason why God put me through this life storm will never be revealed to me. I had been told by several people how their lives were impacted by my trial. Perhaps that was the reason why everything happened to me. Maybe I was supposed to die on October 8, but thousands of God's people came together and prayed for me, and maybe God decided to answer those prayers. If the lesson that I am to learn through this trial is the simple fact that God saved my life, then I am all right with that.

I came across a passage in Isaiah that had a large impact on me. I remember reading this passage several months ago, but I had not remembered it until now.

Isaiah 38: 1–6; 17

> In those days Hezekiah became ill and was at the point of death. The prophet Isaiah son of Amoz went to him and said, "This is what the Lord says: Put your house in order, because you are going to die; you will not recover." Hezekiah turned his face to the wall and prayed to the Lord, "Remember, O Lord, how I have walked before you faithfully and with wholehearted devotion and have done

what is good in your eyes." And Hezekiah wept bitterly. Then the word of the Lord came to Isaiah: "Go and tell Hezekiah, 'This is what the Lord, the God of your father David, says: I have heard your prayer and seen your tears; I will add fifteen years to your life, and I will deliver you and this city from the hand of the king of Assyria. I will defend this city … Surely it was for my benefit that I suffered such anguish.

It was an awesome display of trusting God that allowed Hezekiah to assume that his suffering must have been for his own good. I can only strive to have this kind of relationship with God that would allow me to trust Him in this way.

I know that I am going to trust Him to get me through each day. After all, God took care of me when I was a young child being raised in a one-parent home. He took care of me when I pulled the trigger on a shotgun while protecting my home, only to find out that the bullet was not in the chamber. He helped me find the perfect person to be my wife. Even though the enemy tried to bury me in a state of complacency, God, in His grace, helped me out of that muck while at the same time holding my hand through my grandma's death.

And recently, while I was facing certain death, God listened to the prayers of many and performed what can only be described as a miracle. God spared my life.

Isaiah 48:10

"See, I have refined you, though not as silver; I have tested you in the furnace of affliction."

If you would like to contact the author, please contact him at:
Email: wconger@heartrefined.com
Website: www.waltconger.com

CPSIA information can be obtained at www.ICGtesting.com
Printed in the USA
267472BV00004B/3/P